THE ART OF WAR ON LAND

THE ART OF WAR ON LAND

Illustrated by Campaigns and Battles of All Ages

by

LT.-COLONEL ALFRED H. BURNE

D.S.O., R.A. (RETIRED)

With a Foreword by

MAJOR-GENERAL J. N. KENNEDY, C.B., M.C.

Assistant Chief of the Imperial General Staff (Operations)

WITH 23 MAPS AND 11 DIAGRAMS

METHUEN & CO., LTD., LONDON
36 Essex Street, Strand, W.C.2

TO

GUY BOAS

without whose inspiration this book
would not have been written

First published in 1944

BOOK
PRODUCTION
WAR ECONOMY
STANDARD

THIS BOOK IS PRODUCED IN
COMPLETE CONFORMITY WITH THE
AUTHORIZED ECONOMY STANDARDS

PRINTED IN GREAT BRITAIN

FOREWORD

IT seems to me that a foreword to this book is unnecessary, unless perhaps to recommend it to those who are not as yet acquainted with Colonel Burne's writings. Colonel Burne has not only studied military history for many years, but also has to his credit a gallant and distinguished record of active service. He is therefore exceptionally qualified to interpret both the theory and the practice of the art of warfare.

The present volume represents the essence of his reflections. Its scope is wide and well conceived.

A general knowledge of the principles of war and their modern application should be widespread. As the tempo of warfare grows, with the advance of science, so does the danger of lack of knowledge also grow.

The problem that confronts every great civilized power is that of maintaining its military spirit, its toughness, and its preparedness for war, to enable it to avoid destruction at the hands of less civilized aggressors. The great civilizations of the past did not solve this problem, and they were destroyed in consequence. Until the human race has evolved a happier way of life than, I fear, the present generation will see, it behoves us, if we are to preserve our freedom, to know what war means, and how it is waged. This knowledge in turn will assist to create an enlightened public opinion, without which the nation cannot be prepared to defend itself, and will not make the sacrifices entailed by such preparedness.

In reading Colonel Burne's pages I could not but reflect how much simpler it is to lay down precepts for guidance than to apply them in practice. In the present war it is true to say that all the protagonists have been guilty, at one time or another, of flagrant violation of the greatest principle of all—that of concentration. It is an unpalatable principle in application. There are always so many things that are desirable to do, and so few that are possible to do successfully. To try to do too much is a fatal error—in defence as well as in attack. Yet the temptation, for both statesmen and soldiers, often proves too strong to be resisted.

The assessment of what is possible, and the acceptance of that assessment, present the most difficult problems in higher strategy and in battle alike. In the course of my experience I have been most deeply impressed with the vital importance of this aspect of war, and the disastrous consequences of failure to understand it.

JOHN KENNEDY

5 *Dec.*, 1943

PREFACE

EVEN the most unmilitary person must frequently have asked himself the question during these years of war: Why is one commander successful, another a failure? What is the secret of success in war? In short, what wins battles?

This book is a humble endeavour to find the answer to such questions: in fact, but for its catch-penny nature, I might have adopted "What Wins Battles?" for my title. The problem is a fascinating one, the solution is elusive. The accepted military classics give out confused, halting, and sometimes conflicting answers. But it should be possible, by comparing a series of great victories throughout the ages and noting what battle-winning features they have in common, to arrive at some tentative conclusions. That, at any rate, is the aim of this book.

I have summarized these battle-winning features or elements, and have attempted to classify them in what I have called four Strands of War.

I have also explained and exemplified the terms of strategy. Part I thus becomes an epitome of the whole art of war. The remaining chapters describe a baker's dozen of battles or campaigns which illustrate the conclusions come to in the first chapter. Any selection or anthology lays itself open to criticism, so I may as well say that the considerations that have influenced me in my selection have been that the selected episodes: (1) must be calculated to illustrate the principles of war; (2) must embrace all ages of recorded history; (3) should, where possible, be taken from English history; (4) should be tolerably well known, and the general in command should bear a famous name. This last consideration was largely induced by the desire to avoid an attempted display of erudition (for the same reason the illustrations in Part I are confined to well-known events), but there are three possible exceptions; I have tried to replace poor Cassivellaunus on the pedestal from which he should never have fallen; and I have tried to do justice to those maligned commanders, the Duke of Cumberland and General J. B. Hood.

It might be considered that Part I should more logically be placed at the end of the book, on the accepted military and legal principle: First state your facts, then draw your deductions. As against this, the reader may find it more interesting to hear my conclusions first, and then to check them by the actual event. Others may find Part I rather stiff reading, but they will do well to swallow the pill before the jam.

If asked why I have excluded all reference to Cromwell, Gustavus, Turenne, Charles of Austria, or the odious Frederick, my answer is simple—Lack of space.

To avoid possible misconception I should explain that the space devoted to a particular subject bears no necessary relation to its importance. Generally speaking, the more obvious a fact or factor the less space has been devoted to it. Thus, it is so obvious that an army can neither live nor fight without supplies and ammunition that the matter is not harped on.

The almost complete omission of reference to air power in the following pages is due to the fact that this book deals solely with the changeless and eternal elements of war—strategy as opposed to tactics, leadership as opposed to weapons. Now, aircraft when used in conjunction with ground troops, may be regarded mainly as mobile long-range artillery, and just as the book does not deal with artillery *per se*, neither should it deal with aircraft when used in that rôle.

Finally, the maps. I have a great belief in the graphic representation of military operations. Much time can be saved both author and reader if the *movements*, as opposed to the *static* order of battle, can be represented. I have therefore sacrificed map detail and extreme accuracy to this (what I call) *dynamic* form of map, and I would remind the reader that such a sketch-map has little in common with a map produced by the Ordnance Survey.

ACKNOWLEDGMENTS

Chapter IV, with slight alterations, was first published in *The Army Quarterly*. The narrative portion of the Battle of Poitiers is substantially taken from my article in the *English Historical Review*. The chapter on Atlanta is reprinted from my *Lee Grant and Sherman*, by kind permission of Messrs. Gale and Polden. The chapter on the Polish Campaign appeared originally in *The Fighting Forces*; it has been slightly revised. My acknowledgements are due to Lord Wavell for permission to quote from his Lees-Knowles Lecture.

My very particular thanks are due to Mr. Guy Boas, who not only inspired me with the idea of writing the book but encouraged me throughout and took a tremendous amount of trouble in reading through the greater part of the script, thereby saving me from many pitfalls of style.

To my niece Miss Jean Cowie and to her friends for typing much of the work; to various friends who have read and commented on the book—in particular to Major A. F. Becke, to my brother, Archdeacon Burne, and to Lieut.-Colonel Russell Kennedy;—to Mrs. Stephanie Cholmeley for help on the maps; lastly, to the A.C.I.G.S. (Operations) for his all too kind Foreword, I tender my grateful thanks.

A. H. B.

June, 1944

CONTENTS

SKETCH MAPS

PART I

THE THEORY

CHAPTER ONE

THE STRANDS OF WAR

WAR is an art rather than a science: it is waged between human beings, and involves the interplay of their respective characters. Science does not recognize sentient beings as such. Neither the mathematical table, nor yet the laws of electricity, are respecters of persons. No amount of scientific knowledge will dictate to a full-back his right course when the opposing three-quarters are bearing down upon him; for his course of action must depend largely on theirs, and theirs in turn will depend on the invisible, inscrutable wills and minds of several different human beings; not even the mathematical laws of probability will provide the answer; it is a double-sided problem. And so it is in war.

This realization—that there are two parties in the case—should help to dispel a difficulty that puzzles many students of war. This difficulty concerns the so-called Principles of War. These Principles are nowadays generally agreed to be eight in number, and they will be enumerated presently. But it has been observed that some generals have won battles in spite of transgressing or by ignoring one or more of these principles, whilst other generals appear to have observed them and yet have suffered defeat. How can this be, if the Principles of War are, as we are assured, eternal and unchangeable?

The explanation is that war is a tug-of-war—the result of which depends, not on *absolute*, but on *relative* strengths.

B

Moreover, the observance of the Principles of War is only one of several factors in the winning of wars. These factors may be likened to the fibres or strands in a cord. The total strength of the cord may be regarded as the sum of the various strands. The thicker the strands the stronger the cord. That antagonist whose cord is the stronger should overcome his opponent. An omniscient being could doubtless calculate the strength of the various strands and thus foretell the winner, though even here there are certain incomputable ' variables ', to be referred to later, that may affect the issue.

Assuming that the Principles of War form part of one of these strands, as they do, it is obvious that our cord, though including a weak Principle of War strand, might in the aggregate be stronger than our opponent's cord. In other words, our opponent, although adhering to the Principles of War more closely than ourselves, might on balance prove the weaker.

These *Strands of War* are four in number.

I. The quality and capability of the *commander*.
II. The quality and capability of the *troops*.
III. *Morale*.
IV. *Resources*.

Let us consider these Strands in detail.

1st Strand : THE COMMANDER

His personality : the source of inspiration to his troops, imbuing them with confidence in his leadership.

His knowledge : of **his own forces**, their condition and capabilities; **of the enemy**, a close assessment of their nature, strength, dispositions, and the character of their commander. (Under this heading comes the Intelligence work of his Staff.)

His capacity for planning, in accordance with the Principles of War, and of sound strategy.

IInd Strand : THE TROOPS

Their technical efficiency, embracing physical fitness, skilful handling of weapons, and proficiency in tactical manoeuvring.

IIIrd Strand : MORALE

Everything which inculcates will to victory and sustains the troops in the struggle.

IVth Strand : RESOURCES

Numbers—men and weapons.
Armaments—the quality of weapons.
Supplies—food, arms and ammunition, equipment.
Transport—of personnel and material, dependent on number and quality of vehicles, fuel and roads, railways and airborne facilities.

* * * * *

To classify the above: it will be noted that the first three Strands relate to **moral** or **immaterial** factors, whilst the fourth relates to a **material** factor. Marshal Foch, in his *Principes de Guerre*, maintains that moral factors are variable, whilst material factors are not. While we cannot accept this statement in its entirety, it is true that moral factors, impinging on material factors, can alter their value for better or for worse. A striking example is afforded by the action of the 15th Panzer Division in the last days of the Tunisian campaign of 1943: it deliberately fired away its ammunition into the air, owing to the breakdown of its morale, thereby lowering its material strength as well.

Our four Strands of War, it is to be noticed, can also be classified in terms of **weapons** and their **wielders.** Strands

II, III, and IV between them comprise the **weapon,** while Strand I is the **wielder** of it. The latter is the **leader**, the former are the **led**. The interrelation of the one with the other can best be illustrated by a tug-of-war: the last three Strands represent the weight of the team, its fitness, training, and keenness, while the first Strand represents the coach, who decides on the strategy (which end of the rope to take first) and the tactics (the timing of the pulls). It may be noted, in parenthesis, that this simile of a tug-of-war is helpful in comprehending many aspects of warfare.

ADDITIONAL VARIABLE FACTORS

We have alluded to the existence of certain variable and incomputable factors which may affect the issue. These are of a fortuitous and temporary nature, and can be classified under three heads:

1. *Terrain* (or ground), which varies with the situation but can be computed.

2. *Weather*, which in most countries may vary from day to day, and cannot be computed, but can be guessed at.

3. *Luck*, which cannot be either computed or guessed at, but must be gambled on.

1. *Terrain.* When both armies are in motion the greater will be the variability and the difficulty of computation. In trench warfare, to take the other extreme, the difficulty is reduced to a minimum. The influence of terrain is so palpable that it is unnecessary to devote space to it. To take a single example from the North African campaign of 1943: the open desert of Libya favoured the side that predominated in tanks, while in the mountains of Tunisia and Sicily the infantry became once more the ' Queen of the battlefield '.

2. *Weather.* Modern meteorology has certainly reduced the uncertainty of this factor, but has not eliminated it. After the battle of Alamein in October 1942 our pursuit of the Germans was largely frustrated by the heavy rain. Similarly the abnormally heavy and unexpectedly early rain in December 1942 upset out plans for making forward landing-grounds in Tunisia; thus for weeks fighter cover for our ground troops was almost non-existent. The sudden frost followed by the sudden thaw in the spring of 1944 upset the plans of both Russians and Germans in turn.

3. *Luck.* Though it is no doubt true that luck in the long run pans out evenly, this is not true of a short campaign, still less of a battle. It can, in fact, play a disconcertingly prominent part in the issue. A well-known jingle begins ' For want of a nail a shoe was lost ', and ends, ' For want of a nail a kingdom was lost '. Trivial chances can have surprisingly big results. The chance meeting of one of Napoleon's A.D.C. with D'Erlon's Corps during the battle of Quatre Bras may conceivably have cost Napoleon the battle of Waterloo. The chance aeroplane accident to General Gott at a critical phase of the Libyan campaign may have had incalculable results.

All the little unforeseeable accidents in the course of warlike operations come under the heading of ' luck ', and tend to mar performance and preclude the best result. This is known as *friction de guerre*, a phrase that is generally held to have been coined by Clausewitz. Friction of this sort is by its nature incomputable, yet it must be allowed for in all operations. This is more so in attack than in the early stages of defence, for more movements and combinations of events and persons are involved. But when the defence becomes a retreat, friction tends to impede it more than it impedes the attack, for the defender is now also in movement, and his means of communication of orders, &c., are more likely to be disarranged. It thus becomes increasingly improbable that orders will be carried out, or even received, and the most perfect plan is valueless unless it can filter down to the executants.

General von Arnim may have devised excellent plans to meet General Alexander's final attack in the Tunisian campaign, but he lacked the means to get them through to the troops concerned. How true, then, are the words of the great Baron de Jomini: 'War is not an exact science', and again: 'War is an impassioned drama'. Napoleon put it in much the same way when he said: 'War is essentially a calculation of probabilities'. He realized and took into account this element of luck, when he said: 'I base my calculations on the expectation that luck will be against me'. (Unfortunately for the Corsican, he forgot this admirable counsel in his later campaigns.)

At this point the student may well exclaim in despair: 'War is so evidently a gamble that I do not see the need for mastering its so-called Principles and maxims'. Yes, it *is* baffling; yet, apart from exercising our own reason, we have the knowledge that practically all the great captains of war *have* studied closely the experience of their predecessors and have declared that they have benefited thereby. Since luck does undoubtedly in the long run pan out level, likewise terrain and weather, we are left with those calculable factors which we have termed above the Strands of war. Let us therefore return to them having absorbed this lesson, that owing to the friction of war complicated orders and manoeuvres should be avoided; only the simplest will stand the stern test of war. This is one of the main lessons that burnt itself into the minds of our officers during the retreat to Dunkirk.

The tug-of-war simile can also be applied to these three

Variables. The *Terrain* may be wet or dry, level or sloping. The *Weather* may bring the sun in the eyes of one team so that they cannot easily see their coach, the *Luck* may be against them in the spin of the coin. Moreover, *friction de guerre* may be represented by one of the team slipping and twisting his ankle.

The ground is now clear to examine in greater detail some of the ingredients that go to make up the First Strand—the most significant and interesting of the four.

Dealing first with the personality of the commander himself, we cannot do better than quote from the Lees Knowles lectures delivered by Field-Marshal Lord Wavell in 1939. The lecturer gave as the first essential of a general ' the quality of robustness, the ability to stand the shocks of war '. Napoleon said much the same thing: ' The first quality of a commander is a cool head, which will judge things in a true light; he should not let himself be dazed by good or bad news '.

All the great captains have shown this equability, this unruffled calm in a crisis. When the Duke of Wellington learnt that his great flank attack at Toulouse had completely broken down he merely shrugged his shoulders and remarked: ' Well, I suppose I must try something else ', which he did, with complete success. In the same vein, the commander must overcome the paralysing uncertainty of what is called ' the fog of war ' or ' the fog of battle '— due to the absence of reliable news, that obscurity of the situation which is such a feature of most operations of war. Modern inventions such as wireless and aircraft have reduced this fog, but they have not dispersed it.[1] Thus, the commander must possess sufficient ' robustness '

[1] An interesting example of the ceaseless ebb and flow of invention and counter-invention is afforded by the artificial production of fog to replace the fog of war dispersed by the aeroplane.

to be able to issue an order that may send thousands to
their death on most inadequate and incomplete information, for 'War is a lottery'. Napoleon's heartless
exclamation ' I do not care a fig for the lives of a million
men ' illustrates this robustness in an extreme form.

The Field-Marshal goes on to analyse the character of
the successful commander:

He must have ' character ', which simply means that he
knows what he wants and has the courage and determination
to get it.   He should have a genuine interest in, and a real
knowledge of, humanity, the raw material of his trade; and,
most vital of all, he must have what we call the fighting spirit,
the will to win.   You all know and recognize it in sport, the
man who plays his best when things are going badly, who has
the power to come back at you when apparently beaten, and
who refuses to acknowledge defeat.   There is one other moral
quality I would stress as the mark of the really great commander as distinguished from the ordinary general.   He must
have a spirit of adventure, a touch of the gambler in him.   As
Napoleon said: ' If the art of war consisted merely in not
taking risks glory would be at the mercy of very mediocre
talent '.   Napoleon always asked if a general was ' lucky '.
What he really meant was, ' Was he bold ? '   A bold general
can be lucky, but no general can be lucky unless he is bold.
The general who allows himself to be bound and hampered
by regulations is unlikely to win a battle.

This necessity for taking risks had previously been
stressed by a passage in a letter written by James Wolfe
when a colonel on the staff in 1757, a passage that has
since become justly famous:

Experience shows me that . . . pushing on smartly is the road
to success;   that nothing is to be reckoned an obstacle to
your undertaking which is not found really so upon trial;
*that in war something must be allowed to chance and fortune, seeing
it is in its nature hazardous and an option of difficulties ;*   that the
greatness of an object should come under consideration as
opposed to the impediments that lie in the way;   that the
honour of one's country is to have some weight;   and that in
particular circumstances and times the loss of a thousand men

is rather an advantage to a nation than otherwise, seeing that gallant attempts raise its reputation and make it respected; whereas the contrary appearance sink the credit of a country, ruin the troops and create infinite uneasiness and discontent at home.

General Robert E. Lee puts it in fewer words:

There is always hazard in military movements, but we must decide between the possible loss from inaction and the risk of action.

Napoleon laconically brings out the same basic idea:

Shuffling half-measures lose everything in war.

Lord Wavell continues:

So far we have dealt with the general's physical and moral make-up. Now for his mental qualities. The most important is what the French call *le sens du praticable*, and we call common sense, knowledge of what is and what is not possible. It must be based on a really sound knowledge of the ' mechanism of war ', i.e., topography, movement, and supply. These are the real foundations of military knowledge, not strategy and tactics as most people think. It is the lack of this knowledge of the principles and practice of military movement and administration—the ' logistics ' of war, some people call it—which puts what we call amateur strategists wrong, not the principles of strategy themselves, which can be apprehended in a very short time by any reasonable intelligence. There are new forces to handle, both on the ground and in the air, with potentialities that are largely unexplored. Some of them were partially exploited in the late War, but have since been greatly improved and extended, some have only recently developed, some are still wholly untried. The commander with the imagination—the genius, in fact—to use the new forces may have his name written among the ' great captains '. But he will not win that title lightly or easily; consider for a moment the qualifications he will require. On the ground he will have to handle forces moving at a speed and ranging at a distance far exceeding that of the most mobile cavalry of the past; a study of naval strategy and tactics as well as those of cavalry will be essential to him. Some ideas on his position in battle and the speed at which he must make his decisions may be derived from the battle of Jutland; not much from Salisbury Plain or the Long Valley. Needless to say, he must be able to handle air forces with the same knowledge as forces on land.

Add to this that the commander's studies must have a background of solid common sense, and a knowledge of humanity, on whose peculiarities, and not those of machines, the whole practice of warfare is ultimately based.

Thus far we have considered the *personality* of the commander. Next we come to his *knowledge of the worth of his own army and that of the enemy*. This may sound an elementary point, yet it cannot be omitted from our survey, especially in view of its essential importance and of its difficulty. The difficulty is due to the fact that we are here mainly concerned with metaphysics, psychology, the *imponderabilia* of war. At the best, the commander can only guess at or sense the capacity of his men to carry out his intentions. Further, this capacity may vary from day to day, even hour to hour. In the second battle of Le Cateau in 1918 some of our infantry were adjudged too exhausted to make any further advance, despite the efforts of their officers; cavalry were therefore sent forward, and as they passed through the front line the foot soldiers rose up, cheered, and took up the advance again. The commander therefore requires great knowledge of human nature, and as far as possible personal knowledge of his own men. All this must be superimposed on his knowledge of the material conditions— 'the logistics' of the situation, as pointed out by Lord Wavell.

Knowledge of the enemy is also an elementary requisite, and a still more difficult one to acquire. It is here that the Intelligence Branch of the General Staff comes into play. This information will include knowledge of the personality of the commander. The German manoeuvre which won the battle of Tannenberg depended for its

success on the Russian general Rennenkampf not marching to the help of Samsonov. Now, Colonel Hoffman,
who devised this German plan, had met the two Russian
generals ten years previously during the Russo-Japanese
War, and he was aware of the fact that they were such
enemies that they had come to fisticuffs on the railway
platform at Mukden. He therefore correctly considered
it a legitimate inference that the one would not help the
other. Wellington's victory at Toulouse was due to the
fact that, by dint of much fighting, he had sized up his
opponent Soult, and reckoned, correctly, that he could
take risks with him.

Even the most perfect Intelligence Service will not
manage to disperse the inevitable ' fog of war ' which is
so unnerving to second-rate commanders: it can only
reduce it. Practical experience is of course a help—
Wellington once declared that he had spent most of his
(military) life guessing what was going on ' the other side
of the hill '.

The third heading under which we are considering the
commander is his *capacity for planning* in accordance with
the Principles of War, and of sound strategy. We will,
first, consider the so-called Principles of War, which
require a chapter to themselves.

CHAPTER TWO

THE PRINCIPLES OF WAR

PEDANTS have objected to the use of the word ' Principles ', and it is true that some of the so-called principles
are more in the nature of axioms; that is to say, they
are almost self-evident. But ' what's in a name? ' The
important thing is that they are broad considerations

which have generally proved sound in practice, and commanders will ignore or transgress them at their peril.

The officially recognized Principles are eight in number:

MAINTENANCE OF THE OBJECTIVE
OFFENSIVE ACTION
SURPRISE
CONCENTRATION
ECONOMY OF FORCE
SECURITY
MOBILITY
CO-OPERATION

Let us consider each in turn.

MAINTENANCE OF THE OBJECTIVE

This merely means that the commander must not be ' led off at a tangent ', expending strength on unessential objectives, chopping and changing his plans as his affairs appear to fluctuate from day to day, and even from hour to hour. ' Keep your eye to the main chance.' ' I see only one thing—the enemy's main army,' said Napoleon. The battle of Alamein affords a good example of this. A large pocket of Germans was surrounded on the northern flank, but General Montgomery refused to be drawn into a decisive action at that point, but continued to concentrate his spearhead against the German main force—namely, the Panzer divisions.

The essential objective of an army taking the offensive is the hostile main army. The temptation frequently arises to go for a geographical objective, perhaps the enemy's capital, but if the enemy's main army in the field is defeated, geographical objects will fall inevitably, whilst the converse is not necessarily true. In the Boer

War we captured the enemy's capital, Pretoria, before the main Boer army had been thoroughly crushed—and the war dragged on for another two years. The Germans correctly observed the principle in their Polish campaign; they merely ' contained ' the Polish capital Warsaw, whilst concentrating all available forces for the defeat of the Polish army still in the field. After that was accomplished the capital fell as a matter of course. Sherman in the American Civil War, brilliant in many ways, missed many a chance of defeating his opponents owing to his predilection for geographical objectives.

OFFENSIVE ACTION

It should be obvious that no decision can be expected without resort to the offensive. Passive defence leads nowhere. The earliest known military commentator, the Chinese general, Sun Tzu, said : ' Ability to defeat the enemy means taking the offensive '. But since a school of thought arose shortly before World War II which belauded the virtues of the defence, it may be worth while to tabulate the weaknesses of this form of warfare. ' The defensive ', we are told, ' is the stronger, as well as the more economical form of strategy.' This may have been inspired by Clausewitz, who declared : ' The defensive form of war is in itself stronger than the offensive '. It should be noted that Clausewitz stultifies his case a few lines farther on, where he admits that ' we must only make use of it as long as our weakness compels us to do so ', but the first sentence has earned fame and the second has been overlooked. In any case, modern German writers have disowned this heresy. Bernhardi, a prominent German military thinker of the last generation, wrote in flat and ostentatious contradiction, ' The offensive is the stronger form of war, and has even gained in superiority '.

The sponsors of the new ' school ' seized upon a sentence in the official *History of the Great War* which recorded that odds of about three to one were found necessary in order to ensure success in the attack.   They argued that as we could never expect to attain such odds against Germany, it was fruitless to hope for a successful offensive.   But the sentence in the above work clearly referred to a *local* superiority at the point of attack only.[1]   Now, it is quite easy to concentrate troops in this superiority at one's own selected spot, even though one may be inferior in total numbers.   Indeed, this is precisely what Ludendorff accomplished in his great attack of March 1918; he amassed a local superiority of just three to one, though along the whole front the Germans were in a slight inferiority.

The inherent weakness of the defence is well brought out by Major-General H. Rowan Robinson in his book *Imperial Defence :*

At first sight the chances would appear to favour the defender; for he can remain still, he can dig, he can shoot accurately; whereas the assailant, while on the move, is dangerously exposed and can do none of these things.   The latter, however, has important advantages on his side.   The forward rush, the excitement, a goal to win, combine to give him a moral uplift wholly lacking in the defender, who is always looking to right and left, anxious lest his flanks be turned and communications severed.   The assailant, especially against a passive defence, has freedom of action and power of manoeuvre, and can accordingly concentrate superior forces against any selected point of his adversary's line, or where the front is not continuous against his flanks and rear.[2]

[1] The author has had the personal assurance of the Official Historian that such was his meaning.   It is a well-known fact that we never attained a *total* superiority over the Germans of anything approaching three to one.

[2] *Imperial Defence* (Frederick Muller), by Major-General H. Rowan Robinson, p. 20.   The whole book is strongly to be recommended.

The list of weaknesses inherent in the defensive is a formidable one. They can be briefly enumerated as follows :

(1) *Morale.* As the last quotation shows, the moral stimulus is on the side of the attacker.

(2) To defend a long line *you must scatter your troops*, but as Napoleon put it : ' If obliged to scatter everywhere you will be strong nowhere '. Mr. Winston Churchill made the same point when he explained the weakness of our defence in the Pacific against Japan in 1942. There was such an enormous perimeter to defend that the effort to defend it all resulted in our being weak everywhere. The same thing was seen on a smaller scale in Sicily. The Italians had no less than eighty-four Coastal Regiments spread out all along the coast, but at no point were they strong enough to put up an effective resistance.

(3) The defence *gives the initiative to the enemy* : a palpable advantage. By means of it the attacker is always ' one move ahead '. ' Time lag ' is inherent in the defence. Watch a boxer or fencer on the defensive : whenever his opponent makes a lunge, whether feint or genuine, there is a split second of time before the defender starts to parry it. It is just the same in war, only more so. Several days may elapse before the defender can concentrate sufficient troops behind the point attacked. By that time the enemy may have switched his attack to a fresh spot which has thereby become denuded of defenders. The bombing offensive on Germany in 1943 is an illustration of this. Cologne, say, would be attacked several days running ; the Germans would hurry reinforcements of A.A. guns to the spot from Hamburg. The bombing attack would then be suddenly switched to Hamburg, and the reverse process set in motion. The Germans were always one move behind.

(4) From the above it follows that the attacker has the

choice of the time and place of the attack. He obviously aims at making both as inconvenient as possible for the defender. This is so palpable an advantage that it requires no emphasis.

(5) The element of *Surprise* favours the offensive. This follows also from the above. Once again it requires no stressing. It is true that the defender may at times produce a modified surprise. A notable example was the action of the French army in Champagne in July 1918. Knowing that an attack was impending, the army secretly evacuated its front line just before the battle, and was able to hold the enemy with surprising force in its second line.

(6) The defence involves a *wastage of troops*. The whole length of the line must be held, but the enemy will probably only attack in one or two spots. The troops holding those parts of the line that are not attacked may never see action at all. Thus the enemy is enabled to concentrate superior force at the decisive point, even though he may be weaker in the aggregate. (This concentration is the governing principle of strategy, as will be made evident later on.) A good example is the wastage of the garrison of the Maginot line in France in 1940. Most of the troops did not fire a shot, whilst their comrades in the field were being outnumbered and overrun. The permanent garrisons of our coast defences are bound to tie up troops that may never actually be employed. In the same way British and Allied troops were necessarily kept unemployed in England, Syria, and Australia in 1941 in case of an attack that in fact never eventuated.

(7) The defender risks the *loss of territory, supplies, civilians*, and potential *allies*. The loss of territory may, as in the Ukraine in 1941, result in loss of grain and food. The loss of supplies such as petrol may immobilize both ground and air forces, as it helped to do at the end of the Tunisian campaign. The loss of civilians, apart from

the tragedy of it, may affect the manufacture of war material, as it did in Russia in 1941. The loss of allies: no small country within reach of the attacker is going to join the defender till it is quite sure it is safe to do so.

(8) The majority of the defender's casualties are a dead loss; the attacker in his advance takes them prisoner and they are thus permanently out of action. But casualties on the attacking side are usually picked up and sent to hospital, where a proportion of them recover and live to fight again. The same applies to material damaged on the battlefield.

(9) The defender cannot afford to lose a single engagement: the attacker usually can. Let him attack in, say, ten different parts of the line; even if he fails in nine of them, but succeeds in the tenth, he has won. But the defender must win in all ten.

It is not to be inferred from all the above that the defensive should *never* be adopted—there are occasions when it is unavoidable—but merely that its inherent weaknesses and limitations are many.

SURPRISE

Again watch a boxer; notice how he feints with his right and hits with his left, surprising his opponent at an unguarded spot. Surprise conveys just such an advantage to its wielder in war. 'Mystify, mislead, surprise your enemy' was the favourite maxim of Stonewall Jackson in the American Civil War. Our two most notable victories on the Western Front in the Great War were largely due to surprise, the battle of Cambrai, and the attack of 8 August 1918—Germany's 'black day'. In World War No. II Rommel failed to secure surprise in his attack at Alamein in August 1942; but a few weeks later Montgomery *did* secure complete surprise as to his point of attack and won the decisive victory of Alamein.

Right through the ages surprise has been recognized as an elementary principle of war. Sun Tzu said: ' All warfare is based on deception ', i.e. on surprise.

CONCENTRATION

This Principle embodies the whole art of strategy, namely: *To concentrate superior forces at the decisive point*. Napoleon worded the principle as follows: ' The art of war may be reduced to a single principle—to unite on a single point a greater mass than the enemy '. We shall see later how he accomplished this himself. In modern days one of the most striking examples was the secret massing of overwhelming superiority opposite the town of Tunis by General Alexander in May 1943. Perhaps the best example from the Great War is the battle of Megiddo. Both will be described in later chapters.

ECONOMY OF FORCE

This Principle merely implies the most advantageous distribution of one's forces. It does *not* imply a mere calculation of the minimum number of men required to win the battle, in order that the remainder of the army can rest behind the line.

Its aim is, on the other hand, to ensure that every man shall play his full part in the struggle. To keep a large reserve well behind the line with little prospect of using it is false economy. Such was the case in the first battle of Gaza in 1917, when our attack was suspended before the reserve had become engaged.

It is difficult to be *too* strong at the decisive point. Nice calculation is involved in the computation of the minimum numbers required to hold that part of the front where no real attack is intended; the balance can then be concentrated at the point of attack, or immediately behind it—the decisive point.

This brings in the question of the *use of the reserve*.   In practice, once both sides have lined up and started the battle, practically the only way the commander can influence the course of events is by the employment of his reserve.   Hence the importance of his decision as to its size and composition, situation, and time of employment.

Both Wellington and Napoleon uttered contradictory remarks about the reserve, at one time or another.   They seem to have agreed that he who retains his reserve in hand the longer whilst inducing his opponent to expend his, will win.   But this quandary arises: if you always keep your reserve intact, of what practical use is it?   It might as well never have existed, and the troops of which it was composed might have been better employed elsewhere; Napoleon said scathingly: ' A general who keeps fresh troops for the day after the battle is almost always beaten '.   On the other hand, directly the general has launched it into the fight he is left without a reserve, and can no longer influence the issue or counter some unexpected blow.

The solution seems to be that the reserve should be freely and boldly used, but that directly that has been done instant steps should be taken to build up a fresh one. It was in this respect that Sir Douglas Haig excelled in the battle of Ypres in 1914.   He was constantly launching his tiny reserve into the battle, and as often scraping together another from byways and hedges.   On the other hand, General von Arnim used up his reserves *before* the decisive attack of 6 May 1943, and was unable to build up a fresh one in time to be effective.

SECURITY

This is an elementary and self-evident Principle.   Indeed, it is so axiomatic that few examples of it will be given in these pages.   The only point to stress is that it is

useless to hope to obtain complete security in passive
defence. It is also unsound. ' He who tries to defend
everything saves nothing ', declared Marshal Foch,
echoing Frederick the Great.[1] It should be noted that
the very act of assuming the offensive imparts a certain
degree of security. Make as if to strike a man, and he
instinctively assumed a defensive attitude. As General
Rowan Robinson expresses it in his *Imperial Defence*, ' The
highest form of strategic security is that obtained through
the imposition of our will upon the enemy, through
seizing the initiative and maintaining it by offensive
action '. There may sometimes be an element of risk
in this, but, as we have seen, war in its nature involves
risk.

MOBILITY

Mobility is not, any more than fire-power or morale,
strictly speaking a *Principle*, but a quality which enables
other Principles—those of *Surprise* and *Concentration*—to be
applied. Its virtues are obvious. It does not necessarily
involve *speed*. Alexander the Great made great use of
Mobility at the battle of Arbela, but there is no evidence
that he excelled the Persians in speed. Of course mobility
may have speed as its essence, where, for example, two
armies are racing for the same objective; for example,
Marlborough and Villars racing for the crossing of the
River Sensée in 1711. But mobility may merely imply
the power to move at all. Example: Hannibal's crossings
of the Alps and of the marshes of the Arno.

The idea of *flexibility* is inherent in mobility; and this
includes *flexibility and elasticity in planning*, and in altering
plans at short notice. Wellington's sudden reversal of
plan at Toulouse, and Montgomery's at the Mareth Line

[1] *Des Principes de Guerre*, p. 49. ' Qui veut tout défendre ne sauve
rien.'

in March 1943, are good examples. To be successful in such cases good and smooth-running staff-work is essential. The greater the complexity of modern war, the greater is the difficulty of maintaining flexibility—especially where amphibious operations are involved. The lack of it prevented the United Nations from taking full and immediate advantage of the unexpected collapse of Italy in 1943. Yet flexibility is one of the hall-marks of the great commander. Said Napoleon: ' Plans of campaign must be constantly changed; according to circumstances, the genius of the commander, the quality of the troops, and the terrain '.

CO-OPERATION

There are two types of *co-operation*: (A) *Internally*; between different arms in the same force. (B) *Externally*; between different forces or armies.

Examples of A. The final battle in the Tunisian campaign, and the battle of Salerno, when not only all arms but all services (army, navy and air) co-operated closely.

Example of B. The battle of Waterloo, which was won owing to the co-operation of the British and Prussian armies.

The advantages in both cases must be self-evident. Since *internal co-operation* is generally concerned with purely battlefield tactics, few examples of it will be given in the ensuing chapters. On the other hand, *external co-operation* merges into concentration, so again few examples will be given.

* * * * *

The above are the eight officially recognized *Principles of War*. But various military writers have advanced others from time to time. Marshal Foch in his *Principes de Guerre* included what he called Free Disposition of Forces (*la libre disposition des forces*) and Liberty of Action (*liberté d'action*). But he did not trouble to elucidate them.

Clausewitz and our own great military writer Colonel Henderson consider *Pursuit* to be a Principle. It is an accepted military maxim that ' touch once gained should never be lost ', and this is especially applicable to the pursuit. To gain the full fruits of victory the pursuit must be vigorous and sustained. It is a curious fact, however, that there have been very few pursuits of this nature in military history. Rowan Robinson goes so far as to assert that ' for 150 years prior to the Great War, Jena, Waterloo, and Tel el Kebir (in the Egyptian campaign of 1882) furnish the only examples of the completion of victory by pursuit '. Going back another century, we can certainly add Ramillies.

All commanders must have been aware of the advantages of vigorous pursuit; hence the mere fact that they did not succeed in achieving it shows that there must be some big predisposing cause militating against its attainment. This cause may be defined as *lassitudo certamine* (to coin an expression), that moral and physical fatigue and reaction that usually supervenes towards the close of a hard-fought struggle as the daylight departs and the pursuit should just be starting. At the battle of Orthez, Wellington thoroughly defeated Soult, but omitted to pursue him. Why? Almost certainly because he was himself wounded just at the close of the action, and his physical and mental powers at that critical moment no doubt suffered temporary eclipse. In the same way Marlborough after his brilliant exploit in forcing the Lines of the Geet in 1705 made no attempt to pursue. He had just taken part himself in a fierce cavalry charge, and was physically *bouleversé*. It is doubtful whether in any army this potential weakness is sufficiently recognized and systematically combated.

Pursuit cannot, however, be elevated into a general Principle, for it is obviously inapplicable in the defence. It is really a strategical or tactical operation.

This brings us to our final section—enunciation and elucidation of the current terms of strategy.

CHAPTER THREE

THE STRATEGY OF WAR

WHAT is the difference between strategy and tactics? The two words are sometimes used indiscriminately to mean the same thing. Most writers on the Art of War have put forward their own definitions, which in itself shows that the task is not an easy one. The difficulty is to define in universal terms the dividing line between the two expressions. Perhaps the following simple definition will serve as well as any: ' Strategy brings the troops to the battlefield: tactics directs their action thereon. Tactics begins where Strategy ends.'

Strategical operations usually have their counterpart in tactics. For instance, the concentration of two armies partakes of the same nature as that of two companies. To this extent battles can be utilized to illustrate strategical principles—and will be so utilized in this book. Beyond this, tactics will not be considered, for they are constantly changing, as the weapons of war change, and in order to be really up-to-date a book on tactics requires revision every few months.

STRATEGICAL TERMS EXPLAINED AND EXEMPLIFIED

Base.—The locality from which an army is supplied. It may be changed from time to time as an army advances, particularly if it is based on the sea. Wellington changed his base twice during the Peninsular War. Montgomery made use of several sub-bases during his advance in North Africa.

Lines of Communication.—The line or lines that connect the army with its base (Fig. 1) ('L. of C.' for short). They may be described as the backbone or vital artery of the army, and form an obvious objective for the enemy.

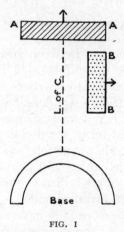

FIG. 1

AA is an army perpendicular to its L. of C.
At *BB* it has formed ' front to its flank '

The Wilderness campaign in the American Civil War was a sustained attempt by the North to cut the L. of C. of the South.

Salient.—A bulge or forward bend in a line of battle, or in a fortress.

Re-entrant.—The reverse of a salient.

To form front to a flank (a useful expression coined by Hamley).—To wheel outwards till the line is parallel, instead of being perpendicular to the L. of C. (Fig. 1). This is a vulnerable position. Avoid it, but induce the enemy to take it up—i.e., protect your own communications whilst threatening those of the enemy.

Example.—Imagine an invading army landing at Hull and advancing on Liverpool. An English army (Fig. 2), based on London, by advancing to engage the enemy at Manchester, would thereby protect or cover its own L. of C. whilst threatening the enemy's. In the Russo-Japanese War the Japanese First Army achieved this by

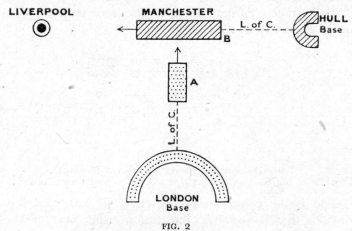

FIG. 2

A protects his own L. of C. whilst threatening *B*'s

its advance on Liao-Yang.[1] The Japanese also benefited by it in their advance down the west coast of Malaya in 1942, for they had the command of the sea, and could thus constantly outflank our troops without endangering their own L. of C. The same applied in our Italian campaign of 1943–44, where also the attacker had command of the sea.

Strategic Flank.—That flank which, if turned, will

---

[1] Those interested will find this point elaborated in the present writer's book *The Liao-Yang Campaign*.

endanger the whole line. In Fig. 1 the right flank of
the position *BB* is the strategic flank, for, if turned, the
whole army must either retreat or have its L. of C. cut.

The Alban Hills formed the German strategic flank
in front of Rome in 1944.

To Outflank.—To extend the line of one's own army
beyond one of the flanks of the hostile army. At the battle
of Arbela the Persian army outflanked the Macedonian
army (Fig. 3).

To Envelop.—To get round the flank, or turn the flank
of the enemy (Fig. 3).

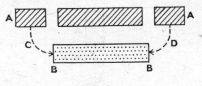

FIG. 3

AA outflanks BB

The envelopment movement *C* turns *B*'s flank
The combination of *C* and *D* is a double envelopment of *BB*

This is the commonest manoeuvre in war, and is so
obvious that it needs no illustration either here or elsewhere in this book.

Double Envelopment or, in current journalism, ' the
pincers movement '. The turning of both flanks. This
may lead to the enemy being surrounded. The classic
example is the battle of Cannae, where Hannibal doubly
enveloped and cut to pieces the Roman army (Fig. 3).

N.B.—This battle was closely studied by General von
Schlieffen, the German Chief of Staff before the Great War,
and he based his plan strategically on double envelopment. But he died shortly before the war, and his plan
was not fully attempted. Schlieffen never intended that
it should be used in conjunction with a war on two fronts.

To Refuse a Flank.—To throw back a flank behind the general line of the army (Fig. 4).

This is generally done in order to thwart an attempt by the enemy to turn that flank. A striking example is the action of Montgomery when attacked by Rommel in August 1942; he threw back his left flank through a right angle, thus completely upsetting the German plan.

Penetration.—As its name implies, this means forcing an entry into some point on the enemy's front. It is the alternate manoeuvre to turning a flank, though *double penetration* may produce a situation similar to envelop-

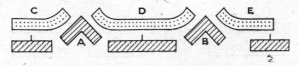

FIG. 4.—Double Penetration

A threatens *C* and *D* with single envelopment
A and *B* threaten *D* with double envelopment
But *A* and *B* are themselves both threatened with
double envelopment

ment. In Fig. 4 the double penetration at *A* and *B* has the effect on *D* of double envelopment.

Single penetration, on the other hand, appears to produce a position of weakness, for it forms a salient, exposed on both flanks. But in actual practice, if the momentum of the attack can be maintained, it has a paralysing effect upon the enemy, whose primary instinct is to protect his own flank rather than to attack that of his opponent. When Alexander attained single penetration at Medjez-el-Bab on 6 May 1943, although it was a perilously narrow one the enemy on the flanks fell back in panic, thus allowing our tanks an unimpeded advance into Tunis itself.

Double penetration can lead to a complex situation. In Fig. 4 *A* is enveloped by *C* and *D*, whereas *D* may feel enveloped by *A* and *B*. On paper the chances may appear even, but in practice it nearly always happens that it is the defender who responds to the threat. If *A* and *B* press back *D* the probability is that *C* and *E* will also fall back, in sympathy, and in order to preserve an unbroken line. The instinct of self-preservation prevails.

Logistics.—The science of moving and supplying troops. The term was invented by Baron de Jomini, but is seldom used in this country. Its application depends upon the resources and tactics of the moment, and consequently does not come within the scope of this book.

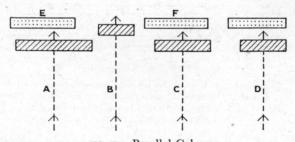

FIG. 5.—Parallel Columns
B automatically turns the flank of *E* and of *F*

Advance on Parallel Lines.—A series of columns advancing in roughly parallel lines abreast.

Its advantages are: (1) simplicity; (2) each column automatically protects the flanks of its neighbours; (3) any gap in the hostile lines will be automatically discovered, and can be exploited by the column that happens to be opposite this gap (Fig. 5).

The Germans tried to employ this manoeuvre in their advance on Paris in 1914, but it was badly applied by some of the army commanders, notably by General Bülow, who called neighbouring armies to his aid, instead of letting them continue marching parallel.

Interior Lines.—Possessed by an army whose L. of C. close inwards.

Exterior Lines.—Possessed by an army whose L. of C. splay outwards.

The first term was invented by Jomini, and adopted by his master and idol, Napoleon: 'As for me I am always on interior lines', the latter once declared.

The study of *Interior* versus *Exterior Lines* is of such surpassing interest and importance that a whole section must be devoted to it.

Thanks largely to Jomini, the belief arose that Napoleon usually employed interior lines and that he won his greatest victories thereby. The truth is that he only won one campaign (his first) by the use of interior lines,[1] and lost the last three campaigns in succession in which he used them. Why, then, it may be asked, was Napoleon so addicted to interior lines? The answer probably is, because a general operating on exterior lines cannot exercise personal control over events: he has to delegate it to his subordinate army commanders. Now Napoleon did not repose trust in his subordinates, but had over-weening faith in himself; this he could best apply by means of interior lines: hence their popularity with him—and hence their popularity almost all through the nineteenth century, which was bewitched by the magic of the Corsican's name. It was not till the Austro-Prussian War of 1866 that Moltke revived the popularity of exterior lines. Even to this day the Napoleonic obsession holds sway in some quarters. But the truth is, as we shall presently see, that with the progress in means of communication—railways, telegraph, wireless, and aircraft—the weakness inherent in exterior lines—namely, difficulty of control and co-ordination—is being rapidly reduced.

[1] I do not agree with those writers who claim that the Ulm campaign was fought on interior lines.

The conditions leading to a situation where exterior lines confront interior lines may take one of the following three forms: they may be static (Fig. 6), dynamic (Fig. 7), or deliberate (Fig. 8). The same general principles apply to all three, so they are grouped together in the exposition that follows.

A study of the campaigns of the last 150 years will show that really decisive results have only been achieved by the use of exterior lines.[1] A campaign fought purely on

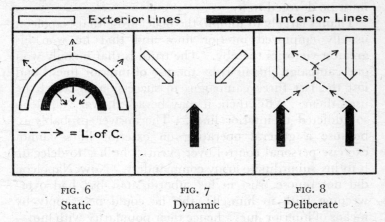

| FIG. 6 | FIG. 7 | FIG. 8 |
| Static | Dynamic | Deliberate |

interior lines, though giving scope for brilliant feats of strategy, does not produce decisive results *unless the enemy's retreat is cut off by the sea or some other impassable obstacle, or unless exceptional speed is used in the pursuit.*

If we consider the conditions and disadvantages under which interior lines operate, the above rather unexpected conclusion need occasion no surprise. For the situation is like that of a boxer pitted against two or more opponents in a ropeless ring. You may drive one opponent into the corner—and he can jump out of the ring, only to

[1] I am not forgetting Napoleon's 1796 campaign, which I do not consider decisive in a purely military sense.

return to it when you have turned your attention to another opponent. This may go on indefinitely, and your prospects of a decisive result are small. If, on the other hand, the ring is roped (represented in strategy by the sea or other impassable obstacle), the prospects of a decision are considerably enhanced.

But other conditions for success are required. The ring must be so large that your opponents cannot strike you simultaneously. You must keep them separated. Further, you must deal with your immediate opponent so drastically that he will not be able to make such a quick recovery that he can strike you in the back while you are tackling Number Two. Whence it follows that the quicker you can swing round on to Number Two, the greater chance you will have of accounting for him before help can arrive.

Applying these considerations to strategy, we can say that for the successful operation of interior lines you require *time and space to manoeuvre*. If either of these is too small you are likely to be overborne by the combined and co-ordinated columns of your opponents. (Speed is an obvious factor in obtaining the requisite time.) On the other hand, if you attack while the space is unnecessarily large, or if you make it too large by pursuing one opponent too far, you may not have time to get back to the succour of the covering troops that you will have left watching enemy Number Two. Very nice and delicate judgement is evidently required. That is the chief problem with which you have to contend. On the other hand, your task is in some ways easier than that of your opponent, for communication, co-ordination, and control are easier, as also the intelligent and timely employment of the general reserve to deliver the final blow. Moreover, if your enemy elects to remain permanently on the defensive, you have it in your power to neutralize his superiority in numbers (if he possesses it) by the rapidity with which you switch your attacking force from one spot on the perimeter to another. It is obvious that it has a shorter distance to move than corresponding hostile columns.

Naturally, if the enemy takes the offensive your difficulties are considerably increased, especially if he advances *all along the line*. In this case you will probably not be able to afford to ignore one of his columns temporarily while concentrating against another. As long as the enemy continues to advance and attack, the advantage inclines to him, and once he has advanced so far that you no longer have *time and space to manoeuvre*, the advantage is entirely on the side of exterior lines. Kesselring just failed to deny us this time and space in the Anzio ' beachhead' in 1944.

We are now in a position to tabulate the conditions and methods favourable to the employment of interior lines.

1. There must be sufficient time and space to manoeuvre (but too much space will defeat your object).

2. The hostile columns must be kept separated.

3. Only one of these columns should be attacked at a time, concentrating superior forces against it.

4. Continue this attack until he has been definitely defeated and disposed of.

5. Always attack somewhere once the enemy has come within reach of your effective blows.

N.B.—1. Decisive results can only be expected if the enemy's lines of retreat are blocked.

2. Speed is the essence of the operation.

The converse considerations apply, generally speaking, to the adoption of exterior lines, which postulate:

1. Superior numbers, because a longer front has to be held actively.

2. Good communications between the various columns.

3. Resolute and bold subordinate commanders of columns.

4. An attack all along the line, all the time.

Lastly, a word of explanation is required of the statement made above that decisive results cannot be expected from interior lines ' unless the enemy's retreat is cut off by the sea or some other impassable obstacle, or unless great speed is used in the pursuit '.

Consider the action of a blacksmith hammering a red-hot horse-shoe. If he holds the shoe up in the air and hits it with the hammer, there will be no appreciable effect. To obtain his effect he must place the shoe on the anvil prior to using the hammer. It is the reciprocal action of hammer and anvil that produces a decisive result.

In war it is the same. The inherent strength of exterior lines is that, from whichever flank you strike, there is on the opposite flank a rope or anvil, in the form of your own troops, against which the enemy can be crushed. But in the case of interior lines this usually is not so. Unless topography (mountains, seas, &c.) comes to our help we cannot expect a decisive result—unless great speed is employed. Why this proviso? Another simile may explain it. Hold up a piece of paper in the air and try to push a pin *slowly* through it. However sharp the point of the pin it will not penetrate, because the paper can bend before it. Now use the pin as a dart; its speed will send it easily through the paper. The resistance of the air to the great speed at which the paper tends to yield to the blow is the substitute for the rope or anvil.

The conclusion of the matter is thus, that the dice are heavily loaded against an army operating on interior lines.

It remains to give some outstanding examples from World War No. II.

On the *European theatre* as a whole we see the Allies on exterior lines, Germany on interior lines:

> *Poland.* Germany exterior; Poland interior.
> *Malaya.* Japan exterior; Britain interior.
> *Tunis.* Allies exterior; Germany interior.
> *Pacific.* Allies exterior; Japan interior.

In all these cases *Exterior Lines* triumphed.[1]

THE RELATION OF POLICY AND WAR

Clausewitz declared that 'War is only a continuance of state policy by other means'. This seems to imply that strategy is entirely subservient to policy. This was controverted by Moltke, who wrote that: 'Strategy works for the object of policy, but is completely independent of its actions'. But in writing thus he ignored the fact that his own strategy had had to give place to policy when policy (in the form of Bismarck) enjoined him to bombard Paris against his soldierly judgement.

This must be so. It is clear that the Government, having fuller knowledge of the conditions abroad than the soldiers, must decide on the theatre of war. It is equally clear that the military commander, having fuller knowledge than the Government of the capacity of his army, should be given as free a hand as possible in carrying out his task. Moreover, no commander should be given a task that he believes impossible of fulfilment.

---

[1] There is, curiously enough, no book that deals at all adequately with this supremely interesting branch of strategy. British writers have scarcely touched it. The most comprehensive treatment probably occurs in *Le campagne d'automne 1813*, by A. G. (Colonel A. Grouard). It has never been translated.

Bernhardi in his *On War of Today*, and Caemmerer in his *Development of Strategical Science* are perhaps the next best authors.

In 1915 the British Government decided that political considerations required the occupation of the Dardanelles, if that were physically possible. Lord Kitchener, as representative of the Government, gave orders accordingly to Sir Ian Hamilton, but refrained from indicating to him how he should carry out his task. This is the correct procedure, and no more need be written on the subject here.

PART II

THE PRACTICE

CHAPTER FOUR

THE BATTLE OF KADESH, 1288 B.C.

THE earliest campaign of which history has a fairly detailed and reliable record happens also to be among the most interesting.[1] Moreover, it illustrates in a striking degree the tenet that ' The principles of war are eternal '.

The accuracy of the main facts of the campaign is vouched for by the fact that they are corroborated from three separate and independent sources. As is only natural when dealing with such an ancient campaign, certain inferences have had to be made in order to render the story intelligible from the military standpoint; but these inferences have been only slight. It is unfortunate that we do not possess the Hittite version of the battle. In its absence we have made due allowance for the exaggeration and embellishment which the Egyptian accounts undoubtedly contain.[2]

[1] The battle of Megiddo, where Tutmoses III defeated the Syrians, is even earlier—1439 B.C.—but the details are highly conjectural, though recent scholarship has made an attempt at reconstruction. In any case the account throws no light on the art of war.

[2] It is only in comparatively recent years that the battle of Kadesh has been studied and the Egyptian records methodically examined. The standard work on the subject is *The Battle of Kadesh* by Professor Breasted (University of Chicago Press, 1903). Where I have departed from his translation and reconstruction of the battle I have generally adopted the translation of the late Professor Eric Peet of Liverpool University, whose help I gratefully acknowledge. It must be clear, though, that the present reconstruction is my own. Where I have departed from Professor Breasted I have given my reasons for so doing in *The Journal of Egyptian Archaeology*, October 1921.

In the year 1289 B.C. Ramses II (father of Menepthah, the Pharaoh of the Exodus) waged war against the Hittites in Syria.   At the conclusion of the campaign he had made good the country as far north as the river Lycus, seven miles north of Beirut. (See Sketch Map 1.) At or near this town he formed a base for the following year's operations, and returned with the remainder of his army to Egypt.

The following spring, being the fifth year of his reign, he took the field at the end of April and, marching through Palestine, reached his base on the coast three weeks later.   Here he organized his army in fighting formation and incorporated the garrison in his force. His army now totalled about 20,000 men, constituted in four divisions, which were named in order of march:—

      The Division of Amon
        ,,   ,,   ,, Rē
        ,,   ,,   ,, Ptah
        ,,   ,,   ,, Sutekh

The Base troops [1] were placed in the centre of the army, while Pharaoh himself took up his position with the vanguard of Amon.   His army consisted of about equal proportions of infantry and chariotry.   The infantry was for the most part armed with spears and shields, and the chariotry wielded bows and arrows.   Whilst, of course, the army would largely live on the country, the troops also took with them goats, sheep, and cattle.   Each division was a force of all arms and was self-contained. The march discipline and the morale were good.   The fame and prestige of the young Pharaoh (he was only thirty) were considerable, and may be compared with

[1] Some authorities describe them as ' Recruits ', or ' Young men '. It comes to much the same thing.

that of our King Henry VIII in his campaign in France in 1513.

It is now time to turn to the Hittites, whose home was in Asia Minor. The opening of the campaign found them grouped about Hamah, with their advanced base at Aleppo, nearly 100 miles farther north. The King of the Hittites, whose name we do not know, was a doughty adversary, and his army was no whit inferior in size to that of Ramses, whilst at least half of it consisted of chariotry (three men to a chariot). The two main armies which were about to become engaged had not met in battle the previous year, and both were imbued with the offensive spirit. We will now leave the Hittite army at Hamah facing south and trace out the course pursued by the Egyptians.

Ramses made the briefest possible halt at his advanced base, and continued his march at the same rapid pace that had characterized the first portion of it. Crossing the mountain chain by a pass to the east of Beirut, he reached the upper waters of the Orontes; thence, marching down the valley along what must be one of the oldest roads in history, he arrived at Kamu, thirty days after setting out from Egypt. In this time he had covered no less than 400 miles, averaging thirteen miles a day, a remarkable record. Here at Kamu, high up above the river bed, he pitched his camp for the night, not yet having come into contact with, or received any intelligence of, the enemy.

Everything pointed to the fact that the Hittites were still far away to the north. The walled city of Kadesh was now fifteen miles distant, and Ramses decided to make that his next day's stage. Starting early next morning, for there was no water to be obtained in the camp high up in the hills, he marched rapidly downhill through Ribleh into the broad flat plain of the lower

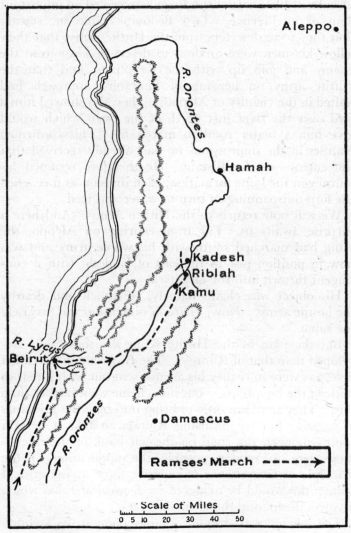

SKETCH MAP I.—Kadesh—Ramses' March

Orontes.   Just short of this town he received an important
item of intelligence.   Two Bedouins came in, stating
that they were deserters from the Hittite army, that their
fellow kinsmen were anxious to desert *en masse* from the
enemy and join up with the Egyptians, and that the
Hittite army on hearing of Pharaoh's approach had
halted in the vicinity of Aleppo.   They also showed him a
ford over the river just north of the town which would
give him a better road to march by.   This confirmed
Ramses in the impressions he had already received that
the enemy was far distant.   He therefore resumed his
journey in the same formation, each division as it reached
the ford outspanning in turn to water and feed.

We will now return to the Hittite Army.   And here a
surprise awaits us.   Far from retiring on Aleppo, the
King had marched south with his whole army and was
now in position just to the east of Kadesh, with a contingent thrown into the city itself.

His object was clear—namely, to attack and destroy
the hostile army.   Now, Pharaoh's intention was precisely
the same.

But the plan of the Hittite King was more fully developed than that of Ramses.   The two Bedouin so-called
deserters were in reality his agents, sent out with intent to
mislead the Egyptians.   But the scheme went farther than
this.   They were not only to bring into play the Principle
of *Surprise*, but by inducing Ramses to take a certain
route—namely, the road on the left bank of the river—
they were to render possible the application of the
Principle of *Concentration* of superior force at the critical
point; this would be achieved by *Economy of Force*, which
involves dissipating the enemy's forces.

The scheme was simple (another point in its favour).
The town of Kadesh was situated upon a hill, almost
entirely surrounded by natural water-courses in the sharp

angle formed by the Orontes and a brook coming in
from the south-west. The Egyptians were to be induced
to march along the left bank. When they arrived
opposite Kadesh the Hittite army would be concealed
from view by the hill and the town. The hostile column
would be strung out owing to the two defiles in the shape
of the ford and the forest of Baui a few miles farther north.
As soon as its head was opposite Kadesh, a strong force
of chariotry was to cross the river by a ford two miles
south of the town, cut the column in half, roll up the head
of it, and then engage the tail as it debouched piecemeal
from the forest. It should be noted also that his *Security*
was amply provided for by the river and by the look-out
men posted on the walls of the city.

A pretty trap was set for Ramses: was he going to
blunder into it? We shall see. After watering and
feeding and crossing the ford, each division resumed its
march without incident and in the same order, Ramses
still leading in person. Each division naturally became
strung out in fording the river, and consequently the head
of its column halted on the far side to allow the remainder
to close up. By this means a gap of from one to two miles
appeared between each division. Passing through the
forest of Baui, about three miles farther on, the columns
again lost distance; but on emerging on the northern
side, Ramses, instead of waiting for the division of Amon
to close up, continued the march in single column, as
there was no sign of the enemy, and the brook running
into the Orontes at Kadesh appeared to offer a tempting
camping ground. The head of Amon reached the
projected camp in mid-afternoon, having accomplished
a march of fifteen miles.

Camp was pitched about one mile west of the city and
eight miles north of the ford. Armed men were seen on
the city walls, so patrols were sent out and a zariba of

shields was erected round the camp.   Pharaoh's pavilion
was pitched in the centre of the camp and the division
of Amon began to settle down.   The reliefs furnish us
with realistic pictures of the scene.   From them it is clear
that whether principles of war are eternal or not, certainly
principles of horse and stable management remain un-
changed.   These pictures indicate that the chariots were
parked and the horses picketed out in lines.   Whilst one
stableman was busy ' haying up ', the other sat on a corn
sack eating out of his mess-tin.   A mounted orderly who
had come in late is seen watering his horse outside the
lines prior to tethering him on the lines—' water before
feed '.

Such was the scene of peace, destined to be rudely
disturbed by the arrival of startling intelligence.   One of
the patrols sent out had captured two enemy scouts near
the city walls.   They stoutly refused to impart any
information until they had been flogged.   Eventually
they admitted that the whole Hittite army was drawn up
just the other side of the city.   Ramses was amazed.   He
turned with fury on to his cowering staff, and was in the
act of soundly trouncing them for their bad intelligence
work when still worse news came to hand.

But before going any farther we must study the position
of the opposing armies at this juncture ; they are depicted
approximately in Sketch Map II.   From this sketch it will
be seen in what a hazardous position the Egyptian army
was placed, strung out as it was in a line eight miles in
length whilst the Hittite army was concentrated and ready
to strike.   And strike it did, and to some purpose.   The
Hittite King had timed his action to a nicety.   The
Principle of *Concentration* involves good timing—i.e., concentration at the right place and right time.   Drawing
up 2,500 chariots (7,500 men) opposite the ford and out of
sight of the Egyptians, he flung them across the river and

into the unprotected flank of the division of Rē. The
Egyptians had no flank-guards out, and were taken completely by surprise. The leading chariots charging down
upon them cut the division in two about its centre, and
the following chariots proceeded to roll up the two flanks
thus formed, but especially the northern one. It was at
this point that an officer of the division managed to make
his way into the camp and informed Pharaoh of the
situation.

Now was the chance for Ramses to show his true
mettle. He had disregarded the Principle of *Security*, and
retribution was about to follow this disregard, unless he
excelled himself. Speedily Pharaoh's mind was made up.
There were two obvious and immediate steps to take.
The first step was to hasten the march of the two rear
divisions; this he instructed his Vizier (his ' C.G.S.') to do.
The second step was to organize a counter-attack with
the division of Amon, which he decided to lead in person.
Dashing out of his pavilion, he sprang into his chariot,
which was waiting ready outside. Already the camp had
been alarmed and horses hooked into chariots. But at this
moment the confusion and the panic which was beginning to make itself evident in the camp were increased
by the arrival of some of the fleetest-footed of the fugitives
from the vanguard of Rē. They dashed panic-stricken
into and through the camp, closely pursued by the Hittites;
and, despite Pharaoh's personal exertions, they carried
away with them the bulk of the defenders of the camp.
Only a few infantry stood fast, and in a very short time
the camp was completely surrounded and broken into by
the hostile chariotry. Ramses saw that no object was to
be gained by staying there, so collecting his diminished
band he cut his way out to the northward and managed to
rejoin the remnants of the division.

The camp thus fell a prey to the Hittites, but this very

fact proved their undoing, for instead of continuing the pursuit they turned aside to plunder the camp. This gave Ramses a breathing space, of which he was quick to make use. Rallying his broken troops, he managed to restore some sort of order; and with them he turned upon the enemy in charge after charge. The narrative becomes somewhat obscure and involved at this point, as is not surprising, but the combat seems to have been a confused *mêlée*, consisting of charge and counter-charge, and it lasted for nearly three hours. In the course of it the Hittite King sent a thousand more chariots into the fray, but did not cross the river himself, or commit any infantry to the fight.

What, in the meanwhile, was happening farther south? On receipt of his instructions from Pharaoh, the Vizier sent off a mounted orderly, skirting round to the west, to summon the two rear divisions to the assistance of Pharaoh with the utmost speed. A few minutes later the Vizier evidently thought that he could help best by going in person to bring up the reinforcements. So he got into his chariot and followed in the tracks of the messenger. Keeping outside the fringe of the battle, he came upon the detachment of Base troops just emerging from the forest. He decided on his plan of action and communicated it to them. They were to strike off to the left, and attack the Hittites in the captured camp from the west, whilst he would go back to the division of Ptah and lead it against the camp in a frontal attack from the south. The division of Sutekh was still south of the Orontes—too far distant to intervene in the battle that day. The Base troops moved off, and the Vizier continued on his way in search of the division of Ptah.

The Hittite chariotry had by this time spent itself, and was not in a fit state to meet the onset of the fresh troops who now advanced against it from two sides. Still

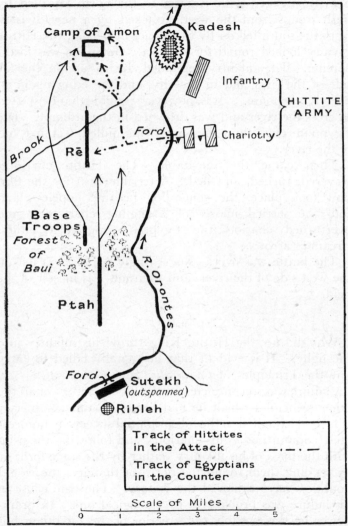

SKETCH MAP 2.—Kadesh—Position at the Moment of the Hittite
Attack

heavily engaged with Ramses to the north, assailed by
fresh troops from the west, attacked by a new division
from the south led on by the Vizier in person, the Hittite
cavalry looked round for support. But none was forthcoming. The infantry remained drawn up on the far
side of the river and in the city, and the King made no
effective response. (It is, however, possible that he started
to cross the river and was drowned in the attempt. The
Egyptian reliefs show the King being pulled, feet first, out
of the river.)

Then came the inevitable. The Hittite chariotry
wavered, turned, and fled. A terrible rush for the ford
now took place, the congestion became hopeless, and
into the serried masses of struggling charioteers and
overturned chariots the Egyptians poured a pitiless
stream of arrows.

The battle was over. Not a single Asiatic was left on
the west side of the river, and Pharaoh was master of the
field.

COMMENTS

Why did not the Hittite King throw his infantry into
the fight? It is evident that he signally failed to carry
out the Principles of *Co-operation* and *Concentration*—and
the failure was so complete as to nullify the effect of all the
other principles which he had been at pains to observe.
If he had exploited to the full his initial success by immediately committing *all* his chariotry and following them up
with the mass of his infantry (either by the same ford, or
by sending them round the north of the city), he would
doubtless have achieved the victory. The true cause of
his failure was probably a psychological one. In brain-
power he was possibly the superior of the Egyptian, but
in nerve he was most certainly his inferior. ' Be prudent
in counsel ', says Bacon in effect, ' and bold in execu-

tion'. The Hittite King reversed the parts, as do so many commanders.

Pharaoh and his Vizier, on the other hand, having transgressed the Principles of *Security*, *Concentration*, and *Economy of force* at the outset, now utilized in striking fashion the very principle the neglect of which contributed to the Hittites' undoing. Ramses II presents a striking and heroic spectacle, fighting in the midst of his enemies for hour after hour against superior numbers, hopelessly cut off from the remainder of his army, without even the means of communicating with them. But his faith in his Chief Staff Officer was supreme, and the Vizier did not fail him: and thus by the observance of the Principle of *Co-operation* together they turned defeat into victory.

But though the victory was a brilliant one it was far from decisive. The Hittite infantry was still intact, and Ramses refrained from pursuing the retreating chariots across the river. Also his losses had been exceedingly heavy. In fact, his equanimity was gravely upset by the battle, and so, far from attempting to follow up his advantage next morning and attack Kadesh, he patched up a hasty truce with the Hittites and marched his army back to Egypt.

Viewing the campaign as a whole, it will surely be agreed that it goes far to substantiate the dictum that ' the Principles of War are eternal '.

CHAPTER FIVE

THE BATTLE OF ARBELA, 331 B.C.

IN the year 334 B.C. Alexander the Great, at the head of a Graeco-Macedonian army, crossed the Hellespont, defeated the Persian King Darius on the Granicus river in Asia Minor, and again the following year on the Issus River (near the modern Alexandretta). Advancing south, Alexander captured Tyre and Gaza, and pushed right on into Egypt. Here he stopped over a year, was hailed as ' Pharaoh ', and founded the city of Alexandria. In 331 B.C. he moved north again, by Tyre and Antioch, and then turned east into what is now known as Irak.

Darius had reformed his army and was known to be somewhere beyond Nineveh (modern Mosul). Thither Alexander turned his steps. Leaving Nineveh on his right hand, he crossed the Tigris higher up and, pushing on, came up with Darius on the banks of the Lycus River (modern Great Zab).

Alexander commanded an army of veterans, well equipped, and imbued with the highest morale and faith in his leadership. The backbone of it was formed by the celebrated Macedonian Phalanx. This consisted of a solid block of heavy infantry, in close order sixteen ranks deep, their primary weapon being the formidable Macedonian pike, 24 feet long. The bulk of the rest of the army consisted of cavalry, though there were in addition some light infantry, archers, slingers, and javelin-throwers, and some ' artillery '—i.e., catapults and *ballista*, of which, however, we hear disappointingly little in the battle. The strength of the Macedonian army is said to have been about 47,000 all ranks; but this is probably an exaggeration. The strength of the Persian host is given as over one million. This is still more clearly an exaggeration. We can assume that it very largely outnumbered its opponents; nearer than that we cannot go—and it does not much matter for the purpose of this study. Darius had collected his army hastily, and the troops were for the most part young, ill-trained, and ill-disciplined, in striking contrast to those of the Macedonian army.

On 26 September 331 B.C., Alexander learnt from prisoners that Darius's camp was only a few miles ahead. He therefore halted his army, entrenched his camp, and gave his men four days rest after their gruelling march. On 30 September he resumed his advance, and soon came in sight of the Persian camp.

Darius had two surprises in store for his opponent—a line of fifteen elephants, and 200 chariots. In order that these latter might manoeuvre the more easily in the clearly impending battle, he levelled the ground in the immediate front of his camp. The idea that Alexander might manoeuvre does not seem to have occurred to him.

The ground over which the battle was to be fought was open and sandy, with little vegetation. The Macedonian camp prior to the battle was on a low line of hills. The Persian army lay a few miles to the south-east, on a fairly flat but rough plain, blocking the road to Babylon and to the heart of the Persian Empire.

Like a prudent general, Alexander made a careful preliminary reconnaissance of the Persian position, and noted the above-mentioned levelling of the ground immediately in front of the Persian army. The significance of this will shortly appear. Returning to his own camp, the Macedonian King assembled his senior officers and delivered to them a heartening message, which he enjoined them to pass on to their several commands.

That done, he retired to his tent for the night. But before he had gone to bed, his Second in Command, a veteran named Parmenio, came to his tent and implored the King to make a night attack upon the enemy. This Alexander refused to do, protesting that such a course was beneath his dignity. As it happened, Darius was expecting just such an attack, and accordingly kept his troops under arms all night. A night attack delivered by the whole army is generally considered a modern conception; this incident proves its falsity.

When morning dawned on 1 October, Alexander deployed his troops. There were points of peculiar interest in his battle formation. In the first place, owing to the great disparity in numbers, the Macedonian army was bound to be outflanked, unless the front was dangerously extended. For this reason Alexander 'refused' both his wings in his original dispositions. Next, and as a further precaution, he formed a second line of mobile troops, very close behind the front line—indeed, almost forming part of it. Its special function was to guard the rear in case the feared outflanking movement succeeded in getting right round to the rear of the army. The line of battle was built up on the Phalanx in the centre; Parmenio was entrusted with the command of the left wing, while the King himself led the right wing. (See Sketch Map 3.)

Darius drew up his immense army in one straight line, infantry, chariots, and elephants in the centre, and cavalry on the two wings. These scythe-bearing chariots were a novel form of weapon to the Macedonians, and Darius hoped for great things from their very novelty—just as we expected (and indeed obtained) striking effects from the first appearance of our tanks at the Battle of the Somme in 1916. Darius proposed to exploit this surprise at the very outset of the battle, by an attack on the Phalanx in the centre of the line. Under cover of the confusion that would thus be caused in the hostile ranks, his cavalry was to charge *en masse* and break the Macedonian centre. Darius posted himself in the centre, from where he would be well placed to witness the forthcoming triumph.

But Alexander had taken due note of all this, and had decided on his counter move. Obviously, to advance straight to his front and engage on the prepared levelled

space in front of the Persian host would be to play into
his enemy's hand. Alexander decided to manoeuvre in
such a way as to bring off the battle on ground less dis-

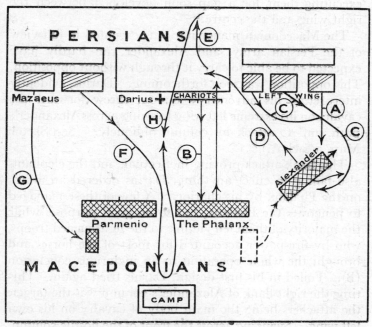

SKETCH MAP 3.—Arbela—Situation at the Moment of Contact
Subsequent main attacks shown thus : ——> and lettered in order :—

A—Abortive cavalry attack
B—Chariot attack
C—Enveloping cavalry attack
D—Alexander's attack
E—Alexander's pursuit
F—Attack on Macedonian Camp
G—Attack on Parmenio's Wing
H—Return of Alexander

advantageous to himself. He therefore advanced not
straight to his front, but obliquely. Resplendent in his
brilliant uniform, he led his right wing in a 'half-right'

direction, aiming at passing beyond the Persian left flank. No doubt the remainder of the army had orders to conform, but difficulty was evidently encountered in executing them, for a gap soon developed between the right wing and the centre.[1]

The Macedonian manoeuvre was executed in full view of the Persian army, and Alexander can hardly have expected to be able to carry it through without opposition. This opposition was soon forthcoming. Darius, evidently interpreting his adversary's design, threw forward the cavalry on his extreme left wing to swing across Alexander's path, and to attack his column obliquely. (See Sketch Map, attack A.) [2]

This flank attack proving ineffectual, and the elephants also failing to effect anything, Darius ordered an attack on the Phalanx by his chariots. A few of these managed to penetrate the Phalanx, but to no good purpose, while the majority of them fell victims to the light-armed troops, who by fire-power accounted for most of the horses and brought the whole operation to an inglorious conclusion (B). Foiled in his first design, Darius tried again. This time the right flank of Alexander's column was the target, the attackers being the main body of cavalry on his own left wing. Swinging across the front of the hostile column, they wheeled to their right and delivered a powerful attack upon the right or rear flank (attack C). But this was the very manoeuvre against which Alexander had,

[1] It is evident that the various commentators on the battle have been puzzled by this manoeuvre, to judge by the diversity of maps that they have constructed to illustrate it. Scarcely two of them agree. I have been content to follow Creasy's reconstruction in my map of the battle in broad outline, showing the main body advancing in line, rather than in column to a flank, though I am aware that so great an authority as General Fuller shows the reverse. I am inclined to believe that it was solely the right wing that moved obliquely to the right.

[2] All capital letters in brackets refer to the Sketch Map.

as we have seen, prepared. His mobile troops of the second line, swinging outwards, charged into the exposed right flank of the Persian cavalry before they could complete their wheel, and put them to flight.

While this cavalry *mêlée* was still going on, a body of cavalry stationed between the Persian centre and left wing went off to join in the fight, thus leaving a dangerous gap between the Persian centre and left wing. With the practised eye of the veteran, Alexander perceived the opportunity thus presented to him, and seized it in no half-hearted fashion. Marshalling all available troops of his own column, and sending orders to the Phalanx to co-operate, he led his troops in person straight against the exposed left flank of the Persian centre (attack D). It was the crisis of the battle.

Whilst his cavalry thus broke into the Persian centre from the flank, the dreaded Phalanx advanced and attacked it from the front. Assailed on two sides with the greatest fury, the Persian centre began to falter. Up till this point Darius had shown ability and coolness; but now his nerve seems to have failed him. Possibly the suddenness and unexpectedness of the attack upset him, for when the Macedonian cavalry drew near, and his charioteer was struck down at his side, the Persian monarch alighted from his chariot, mounted his horse, and incontinently fled, leaving his still fairly intact army to fend for itself.

This was the signal for a general retreat on the part of the centre column, a retreat that was harried and turned to headlong route by Alexander and his cavalry (E).

But a very different scene was being enacted on the other flank. For some time Parmenio had kept his troops out of action. But the advance of the bulk of the Phalanx against the Persian centre had in its turn left an ugly gap.

Into this gap a large force of hostile cavalry penetrated (F), whilst another body under Mazaeus attempted to turn Parmenio's left flank. This latter attempt had been foreseen; by refusing his left—that is, taking up his original formation—Parmenio was able to beat it off (G).

The attack on his other wing, however, met with considerable success. Carrying all before them, the fiery horsemen, intoxicated by success, swept right on to the Macedonian camp, overpowered the guard, and began to pillage it.

Parmenio at this critical juncture sent urgent messages to Alexander, now far away in full pursuit of the hostile centre, appealing for help. To the first messengers Alexander made the notable reply: ' Hold on! The loss of the camp is only a temporary misfortune. Once the main body of the enemy is completely defeated all minor setbacks will be thereby rectified.' But presently further messengers arrived, and whether because he judged that the hostile main body was now irremediably broken, or whether merely to pacify Parmenio, Alexander returned with a portion of his cavalry to the support of his harassed lieutenant.

Meanwhile affairs had taken a turn for the better in the Macedonian camp. That portion of the Phalanx which had not joined in the main attack turned about after the charge of cavalry passed its left flank and followed it back to its own camp. Catching the pillaging cavalry in a state of disorder, the Phalanx had little difficulty in putting them to rout. Thus it came about that while Alexander was falling back towards his own original line the camp pillagers were doing just the same. A totally unexpected clash took place between the two lines. Fighting was hand to hand, and fierce, and lasted a considerable time (H).

Eventually the fight went in favour of the Macedonians,

and Alexander, reforming his horse, resumed his march to the support of the hard-pressed Parmenio.

But by this time Parmenio had routed his opponents, and the whole Persian army was in flight. Wasting no time, Alexander thereupon turned back in his tracks and once again took up the implacable pursuit of the Persian host. In this he was largely animated by the desire to secure the person of Darius himself. But the Persian King had too long a start, and although large numbers of his army were drowned or cut down while crossing the river Lycus, Darius had ridden right on to Arbela, a good twenty miles from the battlefield. Even there he did not tarry, and next day Alexander entered the city, practically unopposed. In a notable passage Creasy thus concludes his description of this, one of the ' decisive battles of history '.

A few days after the battle Alexander entered Babylon, ' the oldest seat of earthly empire ' then in existence, as its acknowledged lord and master. There were yet some campaigns of his brief and bright career [1] to be accomplished. Central Asia was yet to witness the march of his phalanx. He was yet to effect that conquest of Afghanistan in which England has failed.[2] His generalship as well as his valour were yet to be signalized on the banks of the Hydaspes and the field of Chillianwallah; and he was yet to precede the Queen of England in annexing the Punjab to the dominions of an European sovereign. But the crisis of his career was reached; the great object of his mission was accomplished; and the ancient Persian empire, which once menaced all the nations of the earth with subjection, was irreparably crushed when Alexander had won his crowning victory at Arbela.

COMMENTS

This battle exhibits almost as many of the Principles of War as we noticed in the case of Kadesh; and in what we

---

[1] Alexander was twenty-five at the date of the battle, and he died at the age of thirty-two.
[2] Written before the Afghan War of 1880.

have called the battle-winning ' strands of war ' in the
first chapter it is pre-eminent.

Notice first that Alexander had by the time of the battle
acquired the complete and unquestioning confidence of
his men. This is one of the most important attributes
of leadership, and perhaps the most powerful factor in
raising the morale of the troops. For when they have
complete confidence in their leader they are enabled to
' keep their tails up ' when things are looking bad—as they
are bound to do from time to time, even in the best-
conducted campaigns. The campaign of the British
Eighth Army in North Africa in the Second World War
is a classic example of this unquestioning confidence of
the troops in their leader. This confidence feeds upon
success; the difficulty is to acquire it before any success
has been gained. Alexander was born with the proverbial
' silver spoon in his mouth '; our own General Montgomery was not. Therefore his was the harder task.

Notice next the steps Alexander took to stimulate
the zeal and battle-discipline of his troops. Battlefield
orations are common in legend but unfeasible in actual
practice. The general, before the days of radio, could
only address those within earshot of him. Alexander
realized this and, like the Black Prince before Poitiers, he
gave his address to his officers only, but took care to give
it on the previous evening, in order that they should have
ample time to pass it on to all their men.

For the battle itself Alexander was careful to don his
most dazzling armour, and he probably processed down
the line in it, as he had done at the battle of the Issus.
Personal matters of this nature may appear somewhat
puerile, but it is a mistake to despise them. Early in the
morning of one of the most critical days of the Retreat
from Mons in 1914 the sight of Sir Douglas Haig, the
Commander of the First Corps, standing by the roadside,

smiling and meticulously shaved and dressed, had an electric effect on the wearied and somewhat dispirited troops filing past him down the road.

Only the driving power of a great leader, such as Marlborough after Ramillies or Alexander after Arbela, can galvanize the troops into the requisite activity.

The Principle of *Concentration*.—The attack on the Persian centre from two directions is an admirable example of this. The first requisite was the quick, hawk-like eye to recognize the opportunity, the next was the necessary ability and resolution to make use of it. In both these qualities Alexander excelled. The speed and weight of his blow will recur to the mind of the reader when he reads later of Wellington's similar master-stroke at Salamanca. As we have seen in Chapter I, the strategic art of the general can be condensed into this single sentence: ' To concentrate superior force at the decisive point '. The gap in the Persian centre was the decisive point, and against it the Macedonian King concentrated superior forces.

Economy of Force merely implies judicious distribution of the available forces. It is not so easy to be positive in this particular case, but it would appear that all the Macedonians were utilized at one period of the battle or another, whereas the Persian ranks were so heavy and inelastic that many of those in the rear ranks can have taken no active part in the battle, but merely added to the confusion and to the butcher's bill in the pursuit.

Next we come to the ' appreciation of the situation ' by the Macedonian King. About his own troops he was of course well apprised. Of the new Persian army he knew but little; hence he took some trouble in examining prisoners and spent a whole day in reconnoitring the hostile position. It is an old military adage that ' time spent on reconnaissance is seldom wasted '. It certainly was not wasted in this case. The delay incidental to it no doubt reduced the element of surprise, but surprise was in the nature of the case almost impossible to acquire when we consider the huge numbers engaged and the open nature of the country. The result of the reconnaissance was fruitful; it disclosed to the King the prepared space in front of the Persian army, and enabled him to frame his plan to counter it, by means of the oblique or flanking movement of his right wing. It is likely that in this operation Alexander was trying to repeat his flank attack at the Issus, but Darius was too prompt with his counter-attack to allow it full development.

Nevertheless Alexander seems to have accurately divined his opponent's main plan—one of the infallible signs of a great general—and he modified his own dispositions to frustrate it; first, by refusing, or throwing back, his wings at the outset in order to prevent this envelopment; and second, by forming a double or second line, charged with the mission of wheeling rapidly to the rear if necessary and repelling the attacks from that quarter which Alexander quite correctly expected. Thus by elasticity and adaptability Alexander brought to naught his opponent's design.

Let us now glance at Alexander's adherence to some other Principles of War. Take first *Maintenance of the objective*. The Parmenio episode affords a striking example of this. The Macedonian camp was in danger, the left wing was hard pressed, whilst Alexander was driving the Persian main body before him. If he did not return at once there might be disaster in his rear. But the King put ' first things first '. His objective was the main body of the enemy, and for some time he refused to be diverted from this, rightly estimating that if this were completely overthrown any disaster in his rear would be only temporary, and that all would be recovered later. So he carried on the pursuit for the time being, and only when he judged that the decision on his own front was determined did he return (though with only a portion of his force) to the help of his lieutenant. It is further to be noted that Alexander again took up the pursuit, which developed into one of the most inexorable and sustained pursuits in history. It is surprising how few great pursuits have followed great victories—until we consider how exhausted the troops must always be—after a hard day's fight, at the end of the day, when the blood is cooling and the muscles stiffening, and the whole inner man calls out for rest.

The Offensive.—There is something inspiriting about the sight of a small body advancing resolutely to meet a larger one. The stimulating spectacle of David advancing to meet Goliath must have inspired the Israelites, and probably their subsequent victory was largely attributable to it. At the same time it sometimes pays, where the commander can count on the morale of his troops, to allow the enemy to attack first, and to deliver a counter-blow as he reels back. But, first, the troops should be told what to expect and encouraged to meet it; and second, this prompt counter-attack is extraordinarily hard to time and to mount, and there are very few instances of its successful application in history.

Surprise.—As we have seen, the element of surprise was almost impossible to attain. But it seems that Alexander did to some extent attain surprise in his initial oblique and flanking approach. Darius, by preparing the battle arena directly to his front, clearly envisaged the battle taking place on his selected ground; and indeed he was partially successful in this.

Mobility.—The Macedonians had a marked advantage here. They were better trained than the Persians, and were better able to manoeuvre. As regards speed, it is difficult to assess the matter. The Phalanx cannot have moved with great speed in the main attack, but Alexander seems to have deployed his troops for this attack with despatch, and opened it with his cavalry while the Phalanx was closing in on the enemy. Napoleon used to say that the power of an attack is its momentum—that is, *speed* multiplied by *mass*. Judged by this test, the Macedonian attack must have been very powerful.

We have seen in Chapter One that the strands of war are four in number. We have dealt here with No. 1, *The Commander*. As regards the other three, both in *Troops* and *Morale* the Macedonians had the great advantage, whilst in *Resources* the Persians predominated: in particular, his novel weapons—the chariots and elephants—should have given Darius the sort of advantage that the appearance of tanks in the battle of the Somme gave our troops. Nevertheless the effect of this one strand is small in comparison with the other three, which were in combination sufficient to produce one of the most decisive victories in the history of war.

CHAPTER SIX

THE TREBIA AND LAKE TRASIMENE

THE second Punic War opened in 219 B.C. In the spring of the following year Hannibal started his famous march over the Pyrenees and Alps, at the head of an army of 50,000 infantry and 9,000 cavalry. The Romans sent the consul Publius Scipio to oppose him in Southern Gaul, but he arrived too late: Hannibal had already advanced up the valley of the Rhone and had then disappeared. He reappeared in Northern Italy after surmounting almost incredible difficulties and hardships while crossing the Alps. When he eventually emerged in the plain of the Po (Cisalpine Gaul), his army was reduced by a half. Meanwhile Scipio had also moved across to Italy, by sea, and taken command of the Roman troops in that area.

The two armies met for the first time on the banks of the river Ticinus, which flows from Lake Maggiore into the Po near Pavia. (See Sketch Map 5.) A cavalry action ensued, in which Scipio was severely wounded and his troops beaten. Retreating to Placentia, on the Po, he occupied a camp there for some time, whilst Hannibal took up his position a few miles to the south.

Meanwhile the other consul, Sempronius, who was engaged in a successful campaign in Sicily, was called back to help his brother consul and to protect Rome. Whilst awaiting his arrival Scipio vacated his camp at Placentia and moved a few miles south-west on to the west bank of the river Trebia. Hannibal, aware that Sempronius was approaching, did his utmost to bring Scipio to battle, but without avail: Scipio was too wily to be drawn.

The Cisalpine Gauls may be described as neutrals, or the potential allies of which ever side seemed to be the stronger. A number of them came over to Hannibal, and were incorporated in his army. Meanwhile Sempronius, who had reached Ariminum (Rimini) by sea, was collecting and marshalling his army. Marching with great speed, and somehow managing to elude the Carthaginian army, Sempronius effected a junction with Scipio towards the end of December. The combined army was now 45,000 strong, but it contained only 4,000 cavalry—chiefly Gauls, and quite unreliable. Scipio was still out of action from his wound, and Sempronius practically assumed the supreme command.

The Carthaginian army was about 40,000 strong, including a few elephants and 10,000 horsemen. They

were well-trained veterans, and Hannibal had no doubts
of securing the victory if only he could bring his opponent
to battle. The two armies were facing one another
across the river Trebia, now swollen with the winter rains
and snow. The army which fought with its back to the
river would therefore have an obvious disadvantage, and
Hannibal was resolved that it should not be his. He
therefore decided to lure the Roman army across the river.
To do this he kept his own army well back, under cover,
and then sent some Numidians across the stream to harry
the Roman camp and plague the hot-headed Sempronius
into pursuing them across the river. This stratagem was
completely successful. On 26 December 218 B.C., with
snow falling heavily, the Roman army crossed the river
by a deep ford, armpit high, and formed up for battle on
the eastern bank.[1] Hannibal also formed up, and quietly
awaited attack. The crossing of the river was a slow
operation, and evening was at hand when the Roman
army was ready for battle, the infantry being in the centre
and cavalry on the two flanks. Hannibal observed the
same general formation, with this important addition, that
he posted his brother Mago with a force of 2,000 picked
men in the hollow of a ravine on the left flank, where they
were hidden in the undergrowth, thus forming a perfect
ambush.[2] Mago's orders were to lie low until he saw that
the Roman army had shot its bolt and was beset on the
flanks by the Carthaginian cavalry. He was then to strike.

[1] The actual site of the battle is conjectural. Some authorities
locate it on the west bank of the river, but I agree with the majority
in placing it on the east bank.

[2] Polybius, the most reliable authority for the battle, stresses the
skill of Hannibal in preparing this ambush. In wooded country the
Romans had frequently experienced ambushes on the part of the
Gauls, but this was comparatively open country, and Mago made
use of a mere fold in the ground. Roman scouting and intelligence
work were not of a high order, and Hannibal rightly took advantage
of this weakness—on this occasion and later, as will be seen.

All went according to plan. The Roman infantry advanced impetuously to the attack. But although slightly outnumbering the opposing foot soldiers, they were tired, wet, and hungry, whereas the Carthaginians were fresh and had recently fed. The attack on the centre therefore made no impression, and while it was in progress Hannibal launched his cavalry to the attack. They made short work of their heavily outnumbered opponents, who were soon in full flight across the river. But the Carthaginians did not pursue. Admirably disciplined

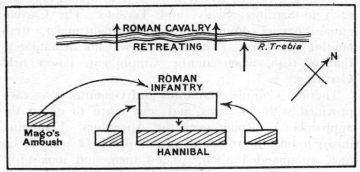

SKETCH MAP 4.—Battle of the Trebia

and trained, they wheeled round inwards against the now exposed flanks of the Roman infantry, while the elephants added to the confusion in the centre of the line.

This was the moment for which Mago had been waiting. Whether on a direct order from his brother, or on his own initiative, he broke out of his ambush and swung right round the Roman infantry and attacked them on their rear face. The combined effect of this concentric attack was decisive: the Roman resistance petered out, and the battle became a slaughter. Ten thousand of the best Roman troops managed somehow to cut their way out and recross the river; the remainder were either killed or captured. The Roman army had almost ceased to exist.

Hannibal did not pursue, for it was already night, and he had every excuse to rest on the field of battle. Thus ended one of the most brilliant of his battles, and the one that he most preferred to dwell upon in his old age.

At Rome the tidings of the battle brought alarm, but not despondency. The Republic stirred itself, and exerted the utmost efforts to repair the disaster. Fresh legions were raised, two of which were sent to Spain, and one each to Sardinia, Sicily, and Taranto. The Carthaginians, having command of the sea, might make a fresh landing anywhere. (The situation was not dissimilar to that of 1943, when another amphibious Power held Carthage.)

The new Consuls, Flaminius and Geminus, were each provided with an army and sent north to guard the approaches to Rome over the Apennines. Flaminius, incorporating the remnants of Sempronius's army in his own, commanded about 40,000 men, and took up a position at Arretium (modern Arezo), whence he could watch the central passes over the Apennines. Geminus with about 30,000 occupied Ariminum, guarding the plain between mountains and sea.

The two armies were to all appearances admirably placed to defend Central Italy and the approaches to the capital, for the main route from the valley of the Po to the south was by the Via Aemilia to Ariminum and thence by the Via Flaminia to Rome. Moreover, the two armies, sixty miles apart, were within three marches of one another, a comfortable distance under the circumstances. Here, then, they rested during the spring months of 217 B.C., feeling happy and secure. But they had reckoned without the formidable Carthaginian. Let us now return to his camp, and note what tremendous plan he was brewing.

Towards the end of March, Hannibal had completed his plans. He had no intention of conforming to his opponent's wishes and expectations and advance by the obvious route. Instead he designed something much more difficult and risky: he would cross the Apennines far to the west, striking over the mountains for the modern Genoa; [1] thence he would follow the coastline for fifty miles, and then strike inland at the flanks of the defending armies. (Sketch Map 5.)

The plan was ambitious—but it succeeded. The great march started at the end of March; the Apennines were crossed without much difficulty; but when Spezia was reached the trials began. It had been a wet winter, the rivers were still swollen, and the ground was marshy and boggy. Ploughing their way onwards, impelled by the iron will of their commander, the Carthaginians eventually reached the marshes on the north bank of the Arno river. Here the floods were extensive, and unexpected. But nothing could deter Hannibal, even though many of his Gaulish allies deserted and went home. The remainder struggled on, wading waist deep through the floods. Ophthalmia broke out, and Hannibal himself lost an eye thereby, and for several days had to be carried in a litter. But still his devoted army floundered on, and eventually reached the ' fair and pleasant highland of Faesulae '.[2]

But of the enemy there was still no sign, though Flaminius's flank was already threatened. From Faesulae,

---

[1] We have no conclusive evidence to indicate the route taken by Hannibal. Some consider he crossed the Apennines farther east, but their reasons are unconvincing.

[2] This flanking march has been compared with that of Napoleon on Piacenza (Placentia), thus turning Beaulieu's position at Valenza. If the Apennines in the one case can be compared with the river Po in the other there is certainly some resemblance.

D

Hannibal could therefore have marched straight on Rome; but his objective was not a geographical one, it was the hostile army; the Romans must be drawn into battle by some means. His first method was to ravage the country all round the modern Florence. Still Flaminius did not stir. Hannibal therefore resorted to a second turning movement. The first movement, up to Faesulae, had covered his own line of communication to the rear. By the new one he abandoned his communications and struck boldly south, past Siena, and thence eastwards till he was directly in the rear of the Roman army. Flaminius's communications with his base being thus cut, he was forced to move out against his opponent. The plan was succeeding. Flaminius marched hurriedly south towards Lake Trasimene, while Hannibal crossed his front, as if making for Perusia. The route took his army along the northern shore of the lake. And here he devised his most celebrated ambush. This time it was on a comprehensive scale: the whole army was employed in it. Just where the road wound along the north shore of the lake there was a level plain, bounded on the north by a line of hills, with two horns running down towards the lake.[1]

In a convenient cleft in the ground slightly to the flank of the first horn, Hannibal placed his Numidians. Beyond the farther horn he pitched his camp, guarding the approach with his cavalry and heavy infantry, while on the hills to the north he secreted the remainder of his army.

Flaminius was headstrong, and inexperienced in war.

[1] Once again there is doubt as to the exact site of the battle. Tourists are shown the battlefield in the plain between Borghetto and Passignano, but I follow the American authority Colonel Dodge, who has made a close study of the ground and places the battle between Passignano and Torre. Not having seen the ground, I offer no personal opinion; but the exact site does not seem to affect the lessons to be drawn from the battle.

Against advice, he would not wait to summon Geminus to his side, but plunged blindly forward into the trap. The battle took place one day in April. A few lines will suffice to describe it. Flaminius advanced straight down the road, the Carthaginian camp being in view in the distance. He had no advanced guard out, nor even, it would appear, scouts. The Numidians were passed

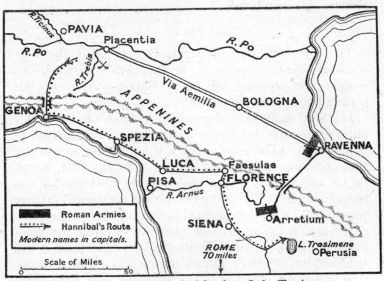

SKETCH MAP 5.—Hannibal's March to Lake Trasimene

without detection, no doubt largely due to the fact that a dense fog lay over the land in the early morning.

The advance continued peacefully and without incident till the second horn was neared. Then the troops defending it rose to their feet and closed to the attack. This was the signal for the remainder of the army: the light infantry dashed down from the hills on the Roman left, while the Numidians rose and sealed up the rear. There was no escape. The Romans were surprised, out-

manoeuvred, and outnumbered.   The battle soon became
a mere butchery.   Flaminius was slain, and after three
long hours the survivors of the proud Roman army broke
and fled.   Thousands of them were driven into the lake
and drowned, ten thousand managed to cut their way
out, mostly in small parties, and the remainder were slain
or captured.   The victors lost only 1,500 men;   the
victory was complete.

COMMENTS

The foregoing narrative should bring out the outstanding military qualities of the great Carthaginian
without the necessity for much elaboration here.   But
certain points must be noted.

It is hard to find any flaws in his generalship, except his
failure to bring Scipio to battle before the arrival of
Sempronius.   The reasons for this failure are so obscure
that criticism is really out of place.   In any case, it can
be advanced that, as the upshot showed, Hannibal was
strong enough to defeat the two armies combined, so there
was no real object to be gained in fighting them separately.

We are on firmer ground when we examine the great
flanking march to Lake Trasimene.   In conception it was
bold and imaginative; in execution it was almost flawless,
thanks in large measure to the inflexible will of the commander, which drove his army forward, however great
the difficulties, much as his great successor Napoleon long
afterwards did, on ground not very distant.   The first
essential in a commander is to forge his weapon, the
second is to have the ability and force of character to
wield it.   In neither of these essentials was Hannibal
wanting.   Throughout his march Hannibal kept clearly
in view his objective—the hostile army.   No geographical
prize, however glittering (and the Eternal City was
certainly that), could deflect him from that objective.

If it be argued that though Hannibal threatened the enemy communications he correspondingly endangered his own, there are two answers. First, though in *theory* the danger is equal on both sides, in *practice* the army that takes the initiative in this respect need seldom be apprehensive of having its L. of C. attacked; the enemy is too apprehensive for his own. Second, the Carthaginian army was largely living on the country, nor did it require the vast ammunition trains that a modern army demands. Hence the risk was not as great as the map would make it appear.

Note next that Hannibal had succeeded in his manoeuvre largely owing to *Surprise*; the very unexpectedness of the operation resulted in its being unopposed. Of the many similar instances of this in military history perhaps the best known is that of Wolfe's ascent of the Heights of Abraham by a precarious goat-path, to win the battle of Quebec. The greater the difficulty the greater the surprise.

Another notable feature of the campaign was the development of the ' intelligence ' branch of the Carthaginian army. By means of spies, by questioning prisoners, by enquiring into and studying the characters of the opposing generals, Hannibal secured a big advantage, of which he made the fullest use.

Coming to the actual battlefields; we find that the decisive element in each was *Envelopment*. Just as in strategy *Exterior lines*, if properly utilized, are of decisive effect, so in battle tactics the same principle produces the same result. That principle we have likened to the principle of the hammer and the anvil. If you strike an opponent who is in a position to recoil before your blow, a decisive result cannot be expected; but if you attack him from two sides, so that he cannot recoil, your blow will have more shattering effect.

Hannibal thoroughly appreciated this, and in all his battles strove to apply it. He did so on the Ticinus; he did so again in the double envelopment movement on the Trebia, accentuated by the rear attack of Mago; he did so with shattering effect at Lake Trasimene; and finally in his crowning victory of Cannae.

The battle of Lake Trasimene is the only occasion in recorded history where a complete army has lain in successful ambush. The sagacity and skill of the great Carthaginian who devised and executed it must have been prodigious. It was the apotheosis of the Principle of *Surprise*.

CHAPTER SEVEN

CAESAR'S INVASION OF BRITAIN

' Cæsar considered he had done enough and need go no further. . . . Everything which had been aimed at had been gained.'

THUS the historian Froude, writing of Julius Caesar's invasion of Britain in 54 B.C. School histories, with few exceptions, have accepted Froude's reading of events. But certain agreed facts do not fit in with this interpretation. It is established that Caesar in invading Kent in 54 B.C. did aim at permanent conquest, but that for some reason he changed his mind after being in the country only seven weeks and that he quitted it incontinently, never to return. It is agreed that the upshot of the expedition, which had raised great expectations, was received with disappointment at Rome; Tacitus wrote that the British ' retained their freedom and were never tributaries to Rome ',[1] while Lucan a century later stated bluntly:

[1] *Annals of Tacitus*, xii. 34. ' Vacui a securibus et tributis.'

' Caesar turns his frightened back on the coveted land of Britain '.[1]

How are we to account for this unexpected setback to the all-conquering Caesar's arms? I hold that the answer can be given in one word—CASSIVELLAUNUS.

The matter is controversial, and this is not the place to establish my thesis.[2] It must suffice to say that all the facts, and most of the inferences, hereunder set forth are supported by one or more reputable historians. My contention is that Cassivellaunus, the British prince, by his sound strategy and adherence to the Principles of War, thwarted the carefully laid plans of the greatest soldier of his age—Julius Caesar.

In 55 B.C. Julius Caesar made what we should now call ' a reconnaissance in force ' of the coast of Kent, landing near Deal, in order, in his own words, ' to learn of their localities, harbours, and landing-places '. Three weeks later the expedition returned to Boulogne, whence it had set out, having learnt nothing about the country except that a landing was possible at the place where it was in fact carried out. Nevertheless Caesar proceeded with his project, spent the winter in accumulating a vast fleet and army, and next summer set out once more from Boulogne to conquer Britain.

It is now time to say something of this coveted land of Britain. The most civilized and most densely populated

---

[1] ' Territa quaesitis ostendit terga Britannis.'

[2] The most detailed and scholarly commentary is T. Rice Holmes's *Ancient Britain and the Invasion of J. Caesar*. But he wrote before the recent discoveries at Wheathampstead, which Collingwood and Myres in their *Roman Britain* (Oxford History) identify with Cassivellaunus's *oppidum*. In some respects I prefer Napoleon III's *History of Julius Caesar*. T. Lewin's *The Invasion of Britain* is also well worth reading. It may be added that Mommsen in his *History of Rome* takes much the same view of Caesar as I do in this chapter.

It is unfortunate that Cassivellaunus was, presumably, illiterate. Caesar's account of the campaign was bound to be one-sided and apologetic.

part of the island was the south-east. In this region the
leading potentate was Cassivellaunus,[1] whose own territory embraced Hertfordshire, the river Lea forming his
eastern boundary. This Prince had recently subdued
his eastern neighbours, the Trinobantes, who inhabited
Essex, had executed their king and banished his son
and heir, Mandubraces. Mandubraces had fled to the
Continent, appeared at Caesar's camp, and begged for
help against his oppressor Cassivellaunus. This obvious
disunity in south-east Britain encouraged Caesar all the
more to persevere with his invasion, and he sent a soldier
of fortune named Commius over to Britain to stir up
trouble and to turn the neighbouring tribes against
Cassivellaunus, their suzerain. In fact he invaded the
country more in the guise of a rescuer than of a conqueror,
much as the Allies did in invading Sicily in 1943.

Only three dates can be definitely fixed in Caesar's
campaign in Britain :

7 July.   The expedition lands.
5 August.   Caesar is back with his fleet on the coast.
29 August. The expedition is about to sail back to
                    France.

In the narrative which follows intermediate dates are
interpolated. These dates are necessarily approximate
only, but should be correct within at most four days.
To assist the smoothness of the narrative the word ' about '
is omitted before each of these dates, but the reader must
understand the limits of accuracy implied.

*   *   *   *   *

On 7 August, in the year 54 B.C., Julius Caesar landed

[1] Not much is known about Cassivellaunus, apart from what
Caesar tells us, but it is known that he continued on the throne of
his country for long after Caesar's departure, that his son finally
subdued the Trinobantes, and that his grandson, Shakespeare's
Cymbeline, further extended his dominions.

on the gently shelving coast of Kent, between Deal and Sandwich, at the head of an army consisting of five legions and 2,000 Gallic cavalry—say 23,000 all told. This army was transported and escorted by a vast fleet of some 800 vessels.

The landing was unopposed, and Caesar, not waiting to beach all his vessels, pushed inland by a night march in search of his opponents, leaving ten cohorts and 300 cavalry—say 4,000 men—as garrison for his base camp.

We must now move across to the other camp, and see what the Britons were doing about the defence of their native soil. The tribes of the south-east were of course apprised of the danger that was about to beset them and had taken steps to meet it. The chief of these steps was to convene a general assembly of the chieftains of the south-east.

This assembly nominated Cassivellaunus as commander-in-chief of the combined forces of the tribes. The Trinobantes had, however, held aloof from this combined movement, and had indeed sent envoys to Caesar, welcoming him to the island and asking him to restore Mandubraces to his lawful throne. This Caesar had undertaken to do.

The approach of the Roman fleet found a portion of the British force, probably under the command of the four Kings of Kent, assembled on the cliffs overlooking the sea. Noting the tremendous size of the armada, this force did not attempt to contest the landing, but fell back inland to the high ground just south of Durovernum (Canterbury). Here Caesar came up with them, after a night march of some twelve miles—rather a remarkable achievement. The British force was in no great strength, Cassivellaunus and the contingents from north of the Thames not having arrived, and after a brief skirmish the men of Kent fell back to an entrenched camp still visible just to the south of Harbledown, hard by the Pilgrim's Way (which probably existed even in those far-off days).

Here took place the first battle of the campaign. Up to date it had been merely a matter of cavalry, but now that his opponents evidently intended to stand and fight, Caesar brought up his Seventh Legion. Marching boldly right up to the entrance of the British camp, the Roman infantry found that it was blocked with *abatis*, constructed of fallen trees. At this moment another body of Britons, who had up till now been concealed in the woods on the two flanks, suddenly issued from hiding and assailed the Romans with missiles of various kinds. But the veterans of the Seventh Legion stood firm and this flank attack was repulsed. Resuming their main task, the Romans pushed right up to the ramparts in a dense column, protected with their shields interlocked above their heads, and managed to throw earth and fascines (or bundles of brushwood) into the ditch till it was sufficiently filled to allow of their crossing. Over the causeway thus made the Romans rushed, and made short work of the garrison. Seeing this, the Britons in the woods retreated, hotly pursued by the Legionaries.

But it was now late in the afternoon; Caesar therefore called off the pursuit and spent the remaining period of daylight in constructing a camp. He was in a hostile and wooded country, and did not feel too happy about his position, in spite of his initial success.

Next morning, 9 July, he sent off a mixed force of cavalry and infantry to resume contact with the enemy. Not knowing in which direction they might be found, he was obliged to subdivide and disperse this force, sending it in three directions. But by this time the enemy had got clear away, and contact was only just being restored when the alarming news reached Caesar that a storm had arisen on the previous night and that most of the ships had been driven on to a lee shore and seriously damaged. Naturally sensitive for the safety of his base, Caesar decided to leave nothing to chance, but to abandon the advance that had started so well, and concentrate everything on the protection of his base. He therefore recalled his troops from the pursuit, and without waiting for them hurried back in person to the scene of the disaster. He there found that no less than forty ships had been totally destroyed and the bulk of the remainder damaged.

The situation was a serious one, but he acted with his customary energy, setting some of his men to repair the damaged vessels while the remainder, after hauling the ships well above high-water mark, constructed an entrenched camp round them.

This work occupied ten invaluable days, and when at last, on 19 July, Caesar set out once more on his march, Cassivellaunus and the outlying contingents with 4,000 charioteers and an unspecified number of cavalry had joined the men of East Kent, and the combined forces were ready to give battle. Advancing by the same road as previously, the Roman army encountered the British on or near the old battlefield.

Caesar's report (the only one extant) of the battle that ensued is substantially as follows. Caesar was in the act of laying out and entrenching camp for the night when his covering troops were attacked by British cavalry and chariots. The first onrush drove the outposts back, but Caesar was able to see what was going on from the camp, which was evidently on commanding ground, and he promptly sent up two cohorts—say 1,000 men—to the help of the outposts. But this force in turn got into difficulties as the Britons deployed more and more men, and there seems to have been something like a panic in the Roman ranks, due to the novelty of the chariots. The sight and the sound of these new engines of war thundering down upon them in line was too much for some of the young legionaries; moreover, they were baffled by the novelty of the British tactics, the extreme mobility of both cavalry and chariots being something new. The latter operated in what we should call extended order, and the slow, dense masses of the Roman infantry were too unwieldy to cope with such an elusive foe. More and more reinforcements were sent into the fray by Caesar, till at length the position was stabilized and the Britons drew off for the night.

That night must have been a time of anxiety for the Roman army, but nothing untoward occurred, and when day dawned Cassivellaunus's camp could be seen some considerable distance away. Although there was some bickering between the outposts of the two armies, Caesar, who was evidently not in the mood to pursue, decided that it would be safe to send out a foraging party to collect supplies. It should be noted that the British had systematically driven all stock away from the route and into the neighbouring woods. Caesar took the precaution of sending an immense escort, three legions and the whole of his cavalry, more than half his army, which seems rather a timorous proceeding.

However that may be, Cassivellaunus was not deterred by the size of the covering force, but boldly attacked it. The Romans had been drawn into some sort of ambush, for they were suddenly attacked without notice from all sides. The cavalry were driven in, and the British continued their charge right up to the serried lines of the legions. It must have resembled the struggle between the French cavalry and the British squares at Waterloo. We do not know how long the struggle lasted, but the Roman legions kept their ranks, and there could be but one end to the story. The British suffered heavy loss, and were in turn charged by the Gallic cavalry. The result, according to Caesar, was decisive, and this time he did not restrain his men in the pursuit. Immediately after the battle Caesar noticed that the Kentish contingents disappeared, and he believed—indeed he stated as a fact in his *Commentaries*—that Cassivellaunus had disbanded them and sent them to their own homes. Fortified by this belief, Caesar continued his march on 21 July, making for the territory of the Trinobantes.

But he was evidently mistaken. A war council must have been held in the British camp and a plan formed, bold in essence and decisive in result. For this, Cassivellaunus the commander-in-chief must be given the credit. The plan was based on three factors. First, the result of the battle had shown that the Roman legionaries constituted a hard core of resistance which it was beyond the power of the chariots to break. Second, the general trend of all the fighting had shown the superiority and greater mobility of the British cavalry and chariotry over the opposing cavalry. Third, the Roman commander had shown great sensitiveness as to the security of his fleet; if that could be destroyed or seriously threatened it might so unnerve Caesar that he might abandon the adventure altogether. The problem was, how to overcome the first factor and exploit the second and third. The ingenious plan devised by Cassivellaunus seemed likely to satisfy all these points.

The allied army was to split into two parts. The Kentish contingents were to remain in Kent and, after Caesar had been enticed away, they were to attack the base camp. Meanwhile Cassivellaunus, with the northern contingents, was to draw the Romans away towards their own country, harassing them on the way, but utilizing their superior mobility to keep out of range of Caesar's main body of legionaries.[1]

---

[1] This interpretation has never before appeared in print nor, so far as I am aware, has it even been mooted. But if my time-table is

This plan was promptly put into operation; the British army divided into two parts, the Kentish portion, under the four Kings of Kent, moved east, while the trans-Thamesian portion, under Cassivellaunus, moved west. We will follow the fortunes of the latter first. Taking the line, in all probability, of the so-called Pilgrim's Way, it would leave it just about Box Hill, and strike north-west for a ford on the Thames now known as Coway Stakes, near Halliford, just above Walton Bridge.[1] Caesar followed somewhat laboriously, being ceaselessly dogged on his flanks by the more mobile Britons, who continued to drive flocks and herds away from his path and to swoop down upon any dispersed parties of foragers. (Sketch Map 6.)

But Caesar drives on as fast as possible in spite of these handicaps. Making on an average seventeen miles a day, he reaches the Thames on 26 July. On the far bank he sees the enemy drawn up covering the ford, with not only a line of stakes in their front, but another line actually in the river-bed. He makes his plan. Sending his cavalry off to the flank, he instructs them to swim the river and attack the enemy in flank; to the infantry he gives the bold order to attack in front, while his missile-throwers (slings and arrows) keep up a heavy fire over the heads of the infantry during their passage through the water. These measures prove completely successful, the crossing is secured, and the march resumed in a

---

accepted it seems the only tenable one. It is absurd to believe that if Cassivellaunus ordered an attack on the base camp approximately four days later he would at the same time have demobilized a great part of his army. It would have been the act of a madman. But he would certainly throw dust into Caesar's eyes if he could, and he seems to have succeeded.

[1] Coway Stakes is the traditional site, and I see no reason to reject it. Various other sites have, however, been propounded from time to time, such as Kingston, Teddington, Brentford, and even Westminster. Rice Holmes seems to incline towards Brentford, on the somewhat slender grounds that stakes have been dredged from the river at that place.

north-easterly direction towards the land of the Trinobantes (Essex).

We will leave Caesar for a moment and go back to the
land of Kent. We must picture the four Kings of Kent re-
ceiving their instructions and disengaging their forces on
22 July. Next day they set out on their return journey to
the coast, and on 24 July, while Caesar was approaching
Box Hill, they delivered the prescribed attack on the
Roman base camp. This camp had been entrenched, was
garrisoned by over 4,000 men, and was probably furnished
with ' artillery '—catapults and ballista (giant cross-
bows). In these circumstances the Kentish kings can
hardly have had much expectation of capturing it,
but, faithful to the orders received from Cassivellaunus,
they made the attempt.

The attack was repulsed by the garrison, but it was
evidently hard pressed, for Quintus Atrius, the commander of the camp, sent an alarmist despatch to Caesar
next day informing him of the attack, and saying that
a further one was expected. On what grounds Atrius
suspected this is not known, but it is likely, for reasons to
be given later, that Cassivellaunus himself was on the way
to join the Kings of Kent, and that news or rumours of this
had reached the Roman camp. Be this as it may, we
must picture the bearer of this sinister news starting out
hot-foot in pursuit of Caesar, while the latter is in the
process of forcing the passage of the Thames. On 29 July
Caesar reached the territory of the Trinobantes, who
promptly threw in their lot with him. They gave the
Roman commander some valuable information; only a
few miles away on the banks of the river Lea, at a place
now known as Wheathampstead, stood one of Cassivellaunus's border posts.[1] This should prove an easy prize,

---

[1] The popular belief is that this was the capital of the Catulauni.
There is no warrant for this belief. Caesar does not state or infer

and two days later Caesar attacked it.   The garrison made
no real effort to defend it and slipped out without losing
any prisoners.   But—and this is the significant point—
Cassivellaunus and his main body were not there to
defend it.   Where could he be?

History does not supply the answer, but it is a legitimate
inference that one of two possible reasons accounted for
the British prince's absence : either he was busy preparing
the defences of his capital, or he had slipped away with a
portion of his forces to rejoin the Kentish Kings and
assist them in their attack on the Roman communications.

Whatever the true explanation (and the latter is the
more probable), Caesar, on 1 August, was aware of two
disturbing facts: first, Cassivellaunus had disappeared;
second, a serious attack had been made upon his base,
and further attacks were momentarily expected.   Caesar
spent little time in making up his mind.   We have seen
how he had reacted to the news of the original mishap to
his fleet; his present reaction was precisely the same.
Taking a flying escort with him, he set out on 2 August
and, travelling at top speed, he reached the base on
4 August.

The news that there reached him we do not know in
detail, but it cannot have been reassuring, for after spend-
ing a few days reviewing the situation, he came to the
drastic decision to abandon an enterprise on which he
had set his heart and lavished so much time, labour, and
money.   He decided, in short, to evacuate the country at
the earliest possible moment.   His official excuses for
this startling step were two : first, the approach of the

that it was.   He merely describes it as ' oppidum ', an entrenched
habitation.   It was on the boundary of their country, on the river
Lea, and was no doubt what we should call a border post.   Who
would select a border post as his capital?   And who would allow the
enemy to take his capital without troubling to oppose him in person
with his main army?

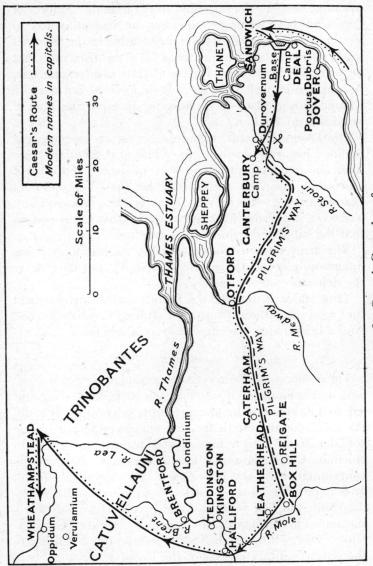

SKETCH MAP 6.—Caesar's Campaign of 54 B.C.

equinox; second, the unsettled state of Gaul. Neither of these can have been genuine, for he had intended to winter in Britain, so the state of the weather in the Channel was irrelevant; and so quiet was Gaul on his return that he was able to disperse his troops into winter quarters. As one writer well puts it: ' It is easy to see that he wanted only a plausible pretext for transporting himself and his army back to Gaul '.

On 9 August Caesar set out on his return journey, and rejoined his army on the 13th. The next few days were spent in patching up some sort of peace terms. He affirms in his *Commentaries* that he took hostages and exacted tribute. He may have taken some hostages, but, whatever the terms, Mommsen asserts that ' it is certain that the stipulated tribute was never paid '.

The army departed in two relays, the last ships being dangerously crowded because Caesar did not dare delay the departure any longer.

Thus ended in unexpected failure and disappointment the most ambitious project of Julius Caesar's career. And a British king was directly responsible for it.

COMMENTS

The dominating feature of the campaign is of course the bold and brilliant plan which deceived Julius Caesar and led to his abandoning the attempt to conquer Britain. We can allot the credit for this achievement with some confidence, for Caesar himself attributes it to the British chieftain Cassivellaunus. The latter may therefore be congratulated as ' the man who spoilt Caesar's destiny '. It is a pity we know so little about him, for he is undoubtedly our first great national hero. If we only knew the date of his birth or death we could celebrate a Cassivellaunus Day. But we must here confine our attention to the purely military aspects of the invasion.

The most striking feature of the British plan is the vastness of conception involved. After suffering a setback in the field, Cassivellaunus, so far from falling back and consolidating, deliberately split up his forces—thereby ignoring the Principle of *Concentration*—and separated the two portions by several days' march. The audacity of the design is almost staggering. Its conception was no doubt due to a correct reading of his opponent's character by the British commander. He evidently had duly noted the Roman's extreme sensitiveness for the safety of his base; for on hearing of the damage to his fleet, Caesar had not been content to leave the repair work to his lieutenant Atrius and his garrison of over 4,000 men—the Roman commander trusted his subordinates no more than Napoleon trusted his marshals.——He must needs hurry back in person and hold up the main body of his army for ten whole days before venturing forward again.

Next, note the successful application of the Principle of *Surprise*. 'Mislead, mystify, surprise.' Cassivellaunus can claim to have done all these. Deftly making a virtue of a necessity, he utilized his setback in the battle of 20 July (pity it has not a name: let us call it the battle of Canterbury) to mislead Caesar into the belief that it was more decisive than it was. The Kentish contingents suddenly disappeared. Probably they purposely spread prisoners' tales that Cassivellaunus had disbanded them. Whatever the method, the facts speak for themselves. Caesar admits that he credited this dispersal, nor would he have ventured to press on into the heart of the country had he realized that he was leaving an intact enemy behind him. Yet only four days later, when the Roman main army was for the time being well out of the way, the Kentish corps felt itself strong enough to assault an entrenched camp occupied by a powerful garrison, and to make such an impression on it that the Roman com-

mander was hastily recalled. Caesar was misled:
Caesar was probably mystified: Caesar was certainly
surprised.

Note next the *flexibility* of the British commander. In
the battle of Canterbury his chariots, in overweening
confidence, had attacked the Roman legions in battle
array, and had been bloodily repulsed. Instantly he
changes his tactics, recognizing, like Fabius Cunctator
when confronted by Hannibal, that a new method must
be applied—that of the guerilla. His troops had shown
their superiority to the enemy's light troops when in
extended order; therefore Cassivellaunus now concentrated his efforts on inducing dispersion in the hostile
ranks and then pounced upon them. These tactics served
their purpose; practically all historians recognize that
Caesar was much perturbed to know how to deal with this
new factor, and in particular with this new weapon, the
chariot, to which his troops were strangers. (The Gauls
had no chariots.) Indeed, he never found the solution,
and he was never able to get to grips with the British main
army for the remainder of the campaign.

The crossing of the Thames is perhaps the most brilliant
operation carried out by Caesar in this brief campaign.
Note the *Co-operation* of all arms—the cavalry turning
movement, probably combined with *surprise* (otherwise
they could scarcely have swum the river unopposed), the
supporting artillery fire, and the bold frontal attack by
the heavy infantry.

It is of interest to consider the question: Would Caesar
have been justified in pushing on to join the Trinobantes
after the battle of Canterbury with his lines of communications insecure? To join up with the Trinobantes,
thereby possibly bringing over some other northern
tribes, was no doubt a tempting project, but it was a
political, not primarily a military one. Now we have

seen that the military must give way to the political consideration where the Government holds it desirable, but it must be understood that if the soldiers proclaim the political end unattainable on purely military grounds, it is not sound to pursue it. When Lord Kitchener gave Sir Ian Hamilton military command in the Gallipoli Campaign of 1915 the latter was bound to acquiesce, as he did, unless he could state on purely military grounds that the project was impossible. In the present case Caesar was for all intents both the Government and the military commander, and it seems that he allowed his military genius to be overridden by his political sense.

Yet another interesting question arises out of the decision to delay his advance for ten days in order to make his base absolutely secure. It raises the age-old problem of balancing the time factor against the security factor. *A* decides to attack *B*. If he waits a few days his army will become fitter for its task; but may not the enemy equally benefit by the delay? Rommel delayed a month in front of the Alamein position before feeling strong enough to attack it seriously; but the month's delay enabled the enemy to benefit by the delay to a still greater extent. On the other hand, Montgomery delayed in front of the Mareth Line, in spite of temptation to strike earlier, until he was in a position to deal Rommel a blow that sent him reeling.[1] There is no Principle of War that will give much help here. A close estimate of the relative logistics of the two sides is the only real guide. This in turn depends largely on the relative efficiency of the Intelligence services of the two armies. The Intelligence service can play a decisive part in the success of the operations. Wellington was badly served by his Intelli-

[1] The ten days pause after the landing at Anzio in February 1944 could only be justified if our strength increased during that period more rapidly than that of the enemy.

gence at Waterloo; thereby over 10,000 of his best troops were absent from the battle, and, had he lost it, his Intelligence service would have been the main cause. But one word of caution.   As pointed out in Chapter One, the 'fog of war' can never be entirely dispelled by the most efficient Intelligence service: 'Something must be left to chance', as Wolfe put it.   'Risks must be taken, and the temptation to make assurance doubly sure in war will eventually lead to retribution.'

A final point. The unexpected appearance of the chariots at first carried all before it.   But, as in the case of the tanks in the Great War, and during bombing in the subsequent one, familiarity breeds contempt, and eventually Caesar discovered at least a partial answer to this new weapon, which was found to lose its terror as the novelty wore off.

CHAPTER EIGHT

THE BATTLE OF POITIERS
1356

POITIERS (spelt 'Peyters' by the Black Prince) was the second of that famous trinity of great victories, of which Crécy was the first and Agincourt the third.   If not so well known as the others, it is from a military point of view easily the most interesting and instructive of the three.   The details, and even the site of the battle, are obscure and controversial.   The grounds on which the following reconstruction is based are given in detail by the author in the *English Historical Review* [1] of January 1938.

[1] The Battle of Poitiers is one of the most controversial of the Middle Ages.   The account of it given here may be described as that of the traditional English School.   There has recently arisen a French School, sponsored by Roland Delachenal in his *Histoire de Charles V,*

In 1356 Prince Edward (afterwards popularly known as The Black Prince) made an extended raid from Bordeaux into the heart of France. Heading for Paris, he turned westwards when approaching the river Loire near Bourges, hoping to join up with an army led by his brother, the Duke of Lancaster, which should be coming south from Normandy. The Duke, however, failed to keep his tryst. Moreover, King John of France was preparing to march against the Prince with a large army. The latter therefore decided to return to Bordeaux with the booty that he had captured in the course of his raid, while the going was good.

---

and tentatively adopted by one or two English writers who have not visited the ground. This is not the place to argue the matter. It must suffice to observe that a study of the ground shows that the French thesis is untenable. According to Delachenal, the English were attacked *en plaine marche* to the rear, in the bend of the river Miausson, which encloses the Champ d'Alexandre (see Sketch Map); the French were facing east, while the English army lined the road from near Bernon to the Gué de l'Homme, facing west. In order to reach his position the French King would have to make a flank march across and in sight of the English front, and then form front to his left—a hazardous manoeuvre of which his unwieldy army was probably quite incapable, landing his force in a sort of *cul de sac* whence it would be impossible to retreat towards Poitiers.

The cause of the controversy is the rhymed chronicle *Le Prince Noir* by Chandos Herald, written thirty to forty years after the battle. According to this account, Warwick's column was south of the river Miausson when the battle opened, as the general retreat of the English army had started. The Herald's account receives only partial support from a recently discovered chronicle, the *Anonimalle Chronicle* (also written a generation after the battle). There can be no doubt that, as given in my narrative, the preliminary steps to continue the retirement were being taken when the French attacked; but I hold that the *Anonimalle Chronicle* does not contradict my reconstruction of the battle. In this connection I am permitted to quote from a letter received from Sir Charles Oman (whose account of the battle in his *Art of War in the Middle Ages* is one of the best and most readable in existence): ' I am quite sure that the only reasonable reading of the battle is that the English fought in a *prepared position*, not when caught on the march and lining up anyhow in a hurry. The battle must be where you put it, and not in the loop of the Miausson.'

But the French King was on his heels and advancing so fast that he caught up the English army in the neighbour- hood of Poitiers. After a curious clash of rearguards, the French army encamped just outside the walls of Poitiers on the night of Saturday 17 September, while the English army lay three miles to the east.

Next morning, Sunday, the Black Prince continued his journey a few miles to the south, watered his horses in the little river Miausson, and prepared to take up a position a mile to the north of it. This position was 1,000 yards in length, and ran along the line of a hedge, rendered famous by the battle, and still, strangely enough, in existence.[1] In front was a shallow valley or depression, with a low ridge beyond. This ridge, called North Ridge on the Sketch Map 7 (which should be consulted here), was covered with a vineyard, through which two tracks led, passing through the hedge and into the English position. Behind the position the ground sloped up gently for 500 yards to a large wood, which in turn dipped down to the valley of the Miausson, 100 feet below.

The English army was about 6,000 strong, including some Gascons and Welsh archers. The French army was between 15,000 and 20,000 strong.

The Duke of Normandy, the Dauphin, commanded the leading division, the Duke of Orleans the second, and the King the third. All were dismounted for the battle except a vanguard, consisting of two bodies under the Counts Audrehen and Clermont.

A truce which had been engineered by the Cardinal de Perigord on the Sunday expired at 7 a.m. on Monday morning 19 September, and as the French showed no signs of advancing, Prince Edward decided to try to slip away. Plans to this end had been made by him at a war

---

[1] My reasons for this surprising claim are given in full in the above- mentioned article in the *English Historical Review*.

council held during the night. The first step was to get the wagons containing the valuable booty on the move. As they drove off, under an escort provided by the Earl of Warwick, they were spotted by the French stationed on North Ridge. Fearing lest the enemy should escape out of their grasp, the two marshals commanding the French vanguard decided to attack at once, Audrehen taking the right-hand track through the vineyard, and Clermont the left.

We must now examine the English dispositions. The sketch map should make them clear. On the right Salisbury's division was stationed, a stone's throw from the hedge. On the left, Warwick's division lined the hedge itself. The archers (dismounted) occupied the first line, with the men at arms, also dismounted, close behind them. The wagons were laagered on the top of the hill to the right rear, close to the road leading down to Nouaillé, where there was a bridge over the river.

Seeing that a battle was inevitable, the Black Prince made an inspiring address to his men. Naturally only a very few could actually hear it, but he took care to order his officers to pass on his words to all ranks. Froissart gives a condensed version of it. A contemporary writer, Baker de Swynbroke, gives a fuller version, which deserves to stand in fame with that put by Shakespeare into the mouth of Henry V on the eve of Agincourt.[1]

*   *   *   *   *

The battle opened with the attack by the French vanguard, which threaded its way through the vineyard and came up against the two gaps in the hedge. That confronting Audrehen was barricaded and occupied; consequently he had no success, and was in fact captured; but that of Clermont met with more immediate success,

[1] See *English Historical Review*, Jan. 1938.

for it came up to the open unguarded gap on the Nouaillé road, and attempted to pass through it and swing to its right in support of Audrehen, already held up opposite his gap. It was only the prompt manoeuvre of Salisbury that frustrated this well-devised operation of Clermont's. Quick to sense the danger, he advanced his line right up to the hedge, thus effectually closing the gap. Meanwhile on the English left our archers were carrying out a notable manoeuvre. As the French cavalry approached, the bulk of them moved still farther to their left into the marsh. Here they were comparatively safe from the hostile horsemen, and were able to gall them with a flanking fire. An obscure passage in Baker describes how the cavalry advanced direct upon the archers, hoping to protect themselves by their breast armour and at the same time protect the infantry following behind them. The English arrows ricocheted off the French breast-plates, and the archers were consequently at a disadvantage till the Earl of Oxford, appreciating the situation, ran down from the Prince's headquarters and directed the archers to shoot obliquely, not at the armoured riders, but at the unprotected hindquarters of their horses. This action was completely successful, and the French attack was repulsed. The struggle had, however, been severe, and in some places (probably in the centre) some cavalry had managed to break through the hedge. Rigid discipline reigned in the English ranks, and no pursuit was allowed. For it was recognized that only the vanguard had as yet been encountered.

The Dauphin's column now advanced on foot. They had shortened their lances from 11 to 5 feet, removed their spurs, and cut off the long toes of their riding-boots, so as to be able to march the better. Their horses were sent to the rear, some say as far as Poitiers. The English men-at-arms had also dismounted, with this difference,

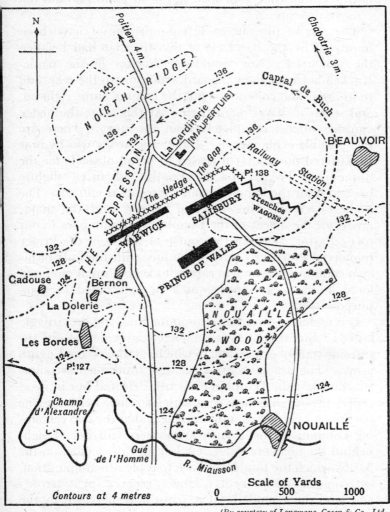

N

Poitiers 4 m.

Chabotrie 3 m.

NORTH RIDGE

140   136   136   Capital de Buch

136

132   La Cardinerie
           [MAUPERTUIS]   136   BEAUVOIR

THE DEPRESSION   The Gap   Railway   Station

The Hedge   xxxxxxxx   P.t 138

xxxxxxxxxxx   SALISBURY   Trenches
xxxxxxxxxxx   WAGONS

WARWICK

132   PRINCE OF WALES   132

128

Cadouse   124   Bernon

La Dolerie   NOUAILLÉ   128

132   WOOD

Les Bordes   124

124   P.t 127   128

124

Champ
d'Alexandre   124

NOUAILLÉ

Gué
de l'Homme   R. Miausson

Scale of Yards

Contours at 4 metres   0   500   1000

(By courtesy of Longmans, Green & Co., Ltd.

SKETCH MAP 7.—Battle of Poitiers

however, that they kept their horses at hand and did not remove their spurs.

The *élan* of the oncoming column cannot have been improved by the spectacle of disaster that had befallen the vanguard. Nor would the impact of the panic-stricken horses of the vanguard, galloping to the rear, add to its order and cohesion. But the column came right on, and seems to have fought well. At this stage the hedge vanishes almost completely from the story. There are two possible explanations. Either the hedge was by now so battered down that it ceased to be an obstacle for the dismounted French, or the English advanced slightly beyond it for the hand-to-hand contest that ensued. The archers were running short of arrows, and the major credit for the defeat of the Dauphin's column goes to our men-at-arms. During the course of this fight the Prince reinforced Warwick's part of the line with the bulk of his own column; but he was careful to keep a small mounted force in his own hands, which he later used to good purpose.

It is useless to attempt to compute how long the struggle lasted; [1] but that it was prolonged is evident from the extreme state of exhaustion to which it reduced the English army. The accounts are clear and frank on this point. When at last the Dauphin drew off, defeated but in good order, the English heaved a sigh of relief, believing the battle was over. From this it is clear that the two remaining columns of the French army were still out of sight behind the northern ridge. A lull now descended on the battle, which the English utilized to replenish ammunition, exchange sound for broken lances, recover spent arrows, and tend the wounded. The pause was increased by the

---

[1] The latest account published in England gives it, with an unwarrantable degree of precision, as twenty minutes. It probably exceeded this considerably.

failure of the Duke of Orleans' column to engage. What exactly happened to it is obscure, but it appears to have been seized with panic and to have fled towards Chauvigny. The Duke of Orleans has of course been unmercifully blamed for this; but it must be remembered that, though the uncle of the Dauphin, he was himself under 21 years of age.

The column of the King of France alone remained. Should he attack, or should he cut his losses and retreat while yet there was time? Retreat would certainly be the more prudent course to adopt, but in those days considerations of chivalry were held of greater account than those of strategy. King John therefore ordered his column forward to the attack.

All the indications point to the fact that during the Dauphin's battle the King's column was a long way in rear. This curious aloofness from the battlefield of King John's column is one of the enigmas of the battle. Whatever the cause, it was undoubtedly the gravest fault committed by the French monarch in his conduct of the battle, though it has been almost universally ignored by the commentators.

There was thus a long distance to traverse, and no doubt the advance was slow, as the knights moved forward on foot. But when the column topped the ridge it presented a formidable spectacle to the exhausted and depleted English ranks. For it was the largest of the three columns, and superior in numbers to its opponents, besides being fresher and better armed.

The English chroniclers are strikingly frank as to the unfavourable moral effect the unexpected appearance of this huge and well-appointed column had upon the Anglo-Gascons. Historians, with that wisdom that comes after the event, have a tendency to regard the defeat of King John's column as foredoomed and inevitable. But there seems no warrant for this. In the first place, the extreme exhaustion of the Prince's army has not been sufficiently stressed. Next comes the moral exhaustion, and reaction that nearly always sets in after a hard-fought fight. The battle was believed to be over.

' The great numbers of the enemy alarmed our men ', says Baker bluntly: the *Eulogium* confirms that ' many of our men were alarmed; nor is it to be wondered at '. . . . *Scalachronica* writes: ' The aspect was so formidable that a large number of the Prince's men retired beyond a hedge '. Baker adds the interesting detail that at this juncture many of our wounded began to leave the field (no doubt ' escorted ' by unwounded comrades, as the custom is!).

No wonder Prince Edward offered up a fervent prayer to Heaven. It was the critical moment of the battle and of his career. Let us consider his perplexing position. He could not at the moment be aware of the flight of Orleans' column, which would be hidden by the North Ridge. He would imagine that he had the main body of the French army still in his front. Should he, in view of the weakened state of his own army, rest content with the blow he had struck against the Dauphin and now fall back? His horses were handy and there yet was time if he was prepared to sacrifice some of his footmen and wagons. Should he accept battle in his defensive position? Or should he take the offensive himself?

Somewhat unexpectedly, when we consider all the circumstances, he chose the third course. Probably two reasons induced this decision.

(1) He had already noted that his defensive position was more effective against mounted than against dismounted men. The latter had fought upon fairly even terms. No benefit was therefore to be gained by awaiting attack behind the hedge.

(2) (The weightier reason.) At the crisis of a battle *moral* superiority may just turn the scale. The Prince's men were then experiencing that reaction after a fight, that *lassitudo certamine* that so frequently supervenes towards the end of a battle, when physical and moral powers are at their lowest ebb. If he was content merely to sit still and await attack, the morale of his troops would scarcely be higher—it might, indeed, be lower—than that of the enemy. But if, with splendid audacity, he ordered an attack—and a mounted attack at that—the old moral superiority of mounted over dismounted men would assert itself and compel victory. The French were in the open, and on the move; they were deficient in archers, and dismounted, and would not be in a good posture to protect themselves against a mounted attack. Some such reasoning as this probably led on the son of Edward III to the dazzling decision which stamps him for all time as a great captain. The depth of discouragement that reigned about him, in contrast to the Prince's own high courage, is well reflected in Baker's story of how a prominent member of the Prince's staff cried out: ' Alas, we are beaten! ' and the Prince's stinging retort: ' Thou liest, thou fool, if thou sayest that we can be conquered as long as I live! '

It is to be noted that the English attack was not to be the purely frontal operation customary in those days. Combined with the frontal attack, Prince Edward arranged a flank attack by the mounted reserve to which reference has already been made. This he placed under the Gascon leader, the Captal de Buch. He was given only a mere handful of men, but the ground was admirably suited to the operation. From Point 138 the ground slopes down gently in all directions. Thus, from the northern edge of Nouaillé wood it is possible to skirt round to the east of the present railway station, and swinging to the left, approach the north ridge unobserved. This was the manoeuvre that was entrusted to the Captal. No precise synchronization of the two attacks was probably either hoped for or aimed at. The final struggle was bound to be prolonged: a few minutes either way would be immaterial. The essential was merely that the frontal attack should precede the flank attack.

From a study of the ground, and identification of the place-names, the final clash must have taken place in the dip in the immediate vicinity of Maupertuis. The final scene must have been a striking one: the English men-at-arms sprang to the saddle, as they had done twenty-three years before at Halidon Hill, and charged down the hill upon the slowly oncoming column of dismounted men. A homeric contest then ensued. It is useless to attempt to give a coherent description of the fight, but certain salient facts emerge. (1) Both sides fought stoutly. (2) The issue was long in doubt. (3) The mounted archers, having exhausted their arrows, joined in the hand-to-hand conflict with their swords. (4) The irruption of the Captal against the left flank and rear of the French column had great—perhaps decisive— effect. In this connection, it seems likely that parties of Warwick's column, returning from the pursuit of the Dauphin, and attracted no doubt by the noise, joined in the flank attack.

The upshot is well known—the capture of King John. In fact, so much emphasis has naturally been placed upon this resounding event that the subsequent remarkable pursuit by the victorious English right up to the walls of Poitiers has tended to be overlooked. But it was yet another of the unusual features of the battle. The pursuers, no doubt, got out of hand, and the Prince had no other means of reassembling them than by hoisting his banner aloft on one of the bushes on the hill-top. There amid the dead and dying he pitched his tent, and there in the midst of his troops he spent the night of one of the most remarkable battles of that or any other age.

COMMENTS

The most outstanding lesson that the battle of Poitiers teaches is the superiority of leadership, trained discipline, and morale over mere numbers.   In these three ' strands of war ' the English army was pre-eminent, whilst the French had the advantage in the fourth strand, resources, with the exception of fire-power, in which—thanks to the long bow—the English were superior.

Let us consider these three ' strands ' in greater detail.

Leadership.   There is a well-defined impression running right through the story that the English commander had a strong personal grip over his army.   From his position on the slope behind the centre of his line Prince Edward could follow with his own eyes the course of the battle, and was thus able to intervene promptly when the occasion arose.   Oxford's mission to the archers is an example of this.   His utilization of the breathing space after the defeat of the Dauphin's column, the decision to mount and attack at the climax of the battle, the pursuit, and the sagacious rallying of his army at nightfall, all betoken generalship of a high order.   To what extent his Chief of Staff, Sir John Chandos, should bear the credit for this, though an interesting speculation, is irrelevant.

The English commander also exhibited an ' eye for country ' in his choice of position.   The reader must take this on trust; only an actual visit to the field would demonstrate it.   But in general we may say that its extent was nicely suited to the size of his army, the hedge crossing and covering the two roads was admirably placed for the purpose, the vineyard immediately in front of the position militated against the mounted attack with which

E

the French opened the battle, the ridge on the right was in exactly the right place to facilitate the covered approach to the French King's left flank, so adroitly made use of by the Captal de Buch, while the slope of the ground upwards behind the position enabled the Prince to exercise visual control of the whole battle.

Discipline. (We use this word in its wider old-fashioned sense—schooling in the art of war, and the will to apply it.) The evidence for this is to a large extent implicit in the above. The orders given by the commander, however good in themselves, would have been fruitless unless the troops were sufficiently schooled in their profession to be capable of carrying them out, and willing to do so. Of this there can be no doubt. There was a certain suppleness, a manoeuvrability about our troops—manifest, for example, in the quick advance of Salisbury's column to the hedge and the Captal's charge—which is in striking contrast with the ponderous, ill-co-ordinated movements of their opponents.

Morale. For ten years the English had held the upper hand in France. In the previous year the Black Prince had led his army all the way to the Mediterranean and back on his ' Grande Chevauchée ', and this year he had led them into the heart of France, acquiring a vast amount of booty, and taking every town he attacked, save only Tours. His troops had confidence in him and unbounded admiration, whilst they held him in a holy awe. It is clear from his somewhat boastful remarks in the course of these operations that he had an equal confidence in himself, and in his army. It is also clear that he realized to the full the paramount importance of morale, as witness the fact that he made a pre-battle oration and took trouble to ensure that it was passed on to the rank and file, just as Alexander had done before him. In short, the morale of the English army was of the highest.

Though certain of the Principles of War, such as *Surprise*, *Concentration*, and *Economy of Force*, were seldom applied in mediaeval battles, there were others which the Black Prince faithfully observed. In the first place, he had a clear idea as to what his *objective* was, namely to get back to Bordeaux with his booty intact. It was only because he reasoned that a battle was necessary in order to secure this objective, that he stood and fought on the ridge above the Miausson river. In this he calculated right; he fought the battle, and then continued towards his objective. It was only by fighting the battle that he could attain that objective.

Note next, that though the battle was, in a sense, forced upon him, and that he was on the defensive strategically, he realized that purely passive defence could not achieve his object. Only by passing to the *offensive* and attacking King John's own column could he ensure that the remainder of his march would be unmolested.

The only point to note regarding *Security* is that Prince Edward was careful to render his baggage wagons secure, by stationing them on a spot whence they had a direct line of retreat, by a bridge at Nouaillé, and that he took care to laager them and to throw up a trench round them for greater security.[1]

As for *Mobility*, we have seen how the English kept their horses close behind them, ready for instant action, whereas the French left theirs well in rear when they advanced. The flanking move by the Captal de Buch is also a good example of the value of mobility. This operation was also instrumental in achieving that *Co-operation* of all arms in the final attack on the King's column. In this grand move all arms combined, the archers mounted as well as the men-at-arms, and gave

[1] This trench was still visible in the seventeenth century.

close support, whilst the cavalry charge on the flank by the Captal was probably the *coup de grâce*.

All was very different in the French ranks. The army had been hurriedly collected, its training was poor, its morale weak and its prestige non-existent. It seemed incapable of manoeuvring: one column was content blindly to follow in the footsteps of its predecessor—or else to run away. The columns were widely dispersed, and King John seemed content to leave it so. Whilst the columns in front were fighting, his own column must have been stationary more than a mile to the rear, in a spot too from which the battle was invisible. (The North Ridge prevented all parts of the battlefield being visible from any point north of that ridge.) The only redeeming feature that we can perceive is that the vanguard and the King's own column fought stoutly enough when it came to the point. But mere courage does not suffice to win battles. That, perhaps, is the most important lesson to be learnt from the famous battle of Poitiers.

CHAPTER NINE

RAMILLIES
1706

IN 1704 the Duke of Marlborough won the great victory of Blenheim. In the following year the French threw up a defensive line known as ' The Lines of Brabant ', forty miles long, protecting Brussels and the Low Countries against the Army of the Allies which had now returned from Bavaria. But by a brilliant manoeuvre Marlborough broke through this line at the first attempt, pushed the French beyond Louvain, and, but for interference by the Dutch Deputies and generals, would in all probability have won another victory to the south of Brussels.[1]

Stung by these repeated setbacks, King Louis XIV strengthened his army in the Low Countries and insisted on its commander, Marshal Villeroi, assuming the offensive in the next campaign.

The Duke of Marlborough heard of this, and was delighted. If the Dutch would not allow him to attack, the only thing to do was to induce the enemy to attack instead. Joyfully on 20 May 1706 he advanced to meet the foe. Both armies were converging on the little village of Ramillies, fifteen miles north of Namur. It was, in effect, a race, and Villeroi won it, arriving in the vicinity of Ramillies on the evening of 22 May.

The French marshal was full of confidence. He believed that his army was vastly superior in numbers, and in nearly everything else, to that of the Allies. (The actual numbers were: French 62,000; Allies 60,000.) His troops shared this good opinion of themselves. It was in this serene spirit that the French army lay down to sleep that night on the open, gently rolling plateau just behind the village that within a few hours was to become world-famous.

Very early next morning, Whitsunday, 23 May, the Allied army moved off in eight great columns. At eight o'clock contact with the French army was gained, and at 10 a.m. the Duke of Marlborough arrived on the opposite heights and saw the French army drawn up before him in a great concave line, four miles long.

The reason for this curious concavity was due to the lie of the ground. Through the village of Ramillies ran a low concave ridge both to right and left. To the south it extended to Taviers, on the bank of the River Mehaigne.

[1] Happily designated 'The unfought Waterloo' by Winston Churchill in his *Marlborough*.

(See Sketch Map 8.) To the north it formed the western boundary to the valley of the River Geete, and extended through Offus to Autréglise. To the east of the river the ground rose again gently, to a slightly greater height than the western ridge. But there was an under-feature, formed by a tiny nameless tributary to the Geete. Between the two streams was a low ridge (marked Gun Ridge on the sketch map), which concealed the nameless stream from the French side. The hollow through which it ran was to play a big part in the battle.

Along the crest of this concave ridge the French army was drawn up, the three villages of Autréglise, Offus, and Ramillies forming three bastions in the line. Villeroi posted himself on the ridge to the north of Offus, whilst Marlborough's battle station was on the opposing height, rather farther to the south. The bulk of the French cavalry were on the right flank, prominent among them being the famous Maison du Roi.[1]

On the Allied side the English had the post of honour on the right. Disguise was impossible: their red coats proclaimed them as they marched slowly down the hill. Villeroi duly noted this, and took the appropriate steps; for Louis XIV had impressed upon him: ' It will be very important to pay particular attention to that part of the line that will endure the first shock of the English troops '. Against the Allied right flank, therefore, Villeroi hastily transferred some of his best troops from his own right. There seems little doubt that this was Marlborough's intention, his plan being to draw off as many troops as possible to the two flanks and then attack the denuded centre.

The battle took the form of a series of phases, some of which merged into and overlapped others.

[1] The Maison du Roi was the Household Cavalry of the Monarch. Its prestige was enormous.

Phase One.—Attack by the two wings. The English troops under Orkney attacked Offus and Autréglise, penetrating the former village, while the Dutch infantry captured Taviers.

Phase Two.—Overkirk's Dutch cavalry attacked the main French cavalry just to the south of Ramillies. The Dutch stood up surprisingly well to the Maison du Roi, but they were outnumbered, and Marlborough, taking advantage of the convexity of his position, was able to transfer cavalry from his right flank to the support of the Dutch with great dispatch. Eventually his cavalry were practically all absorbed in this immense and intense contest, ' the largest cavalry battle of which there is any trustworthy account '.[1] The Duke himself took part, was unhorsed in a charge, and nearly killed or captured. In all no less than 25,000 horsemen took part in this series of *mêlées* which lasted well over an hour. Even more troops were on the way to the decisive point. They consisted of part of Orkney's infantry, which had been withdrawn from the attack, despite his protests, and, taking advantage of the hollow of the nameless stream, were able to approach the centre unperceived by the enemy. But by the time they arrived, the Allied cavalry, assisted by the Danish horse on their left, had gained the upper hand, and the next phase was in full swing.

Phase Three.—The attack on the village of Ramillies by Schultz's infantry, supported by a great battery of guns on Gun Ridge.[2] By five o'clock the village was firmly in our hands, and the Danish cavalry had swept right

---

[1] *Marlborough*, by W. S. Churchill, iii, 116.

[2] The artillery played a considerable part in the capture of the village. Marlborough had massed the greater part of his guns along what I call Gun Ridge in the Sketch Map. The only present evidence that a battle was ever fought round the village is a large hole in a farm building on the eastern edge of the village, which goes by the local name of *trou de boulet*, and which tradition links, no doubt correctly, with the battle.

forward almost to the Tomb of Ottomond.[1]   The French
cavalry all along the southern flank were retreating.
The back of the French resistance had been broken, but
it still remained to turn defeat into disaster.

Phase Four.—The whole Allied line from Ramillies to
the south made a great right wheel, and swept the
French northwards, almost parallel to their line of
battle.[2]   After a pause, the attack was resumed at six
o'clock against the rearguard position that Villeroi was
trying to take up between Offus and Geest.   But it was
too late.   Marlborough had given orders for a general
advance.   It was joyfully obeyed by the English, who
had been sitting on Gun Ridge chafing at their inactivity.
Horse and foot swept forward irresistibly and drove the
remnants of the French army out of Autréglise and Offus,
thereby threatening the left flank of the rearguard
position.

Phase Five.—The whole French army disintegrated, in
a ' *sauve qui peut* ', and the Allied army was launched
into the most implacable pursuit of the eighteenth century.
Marlborough did not himself halt till he was over
twelve miles from the battlefield, having been nineteen
hours in the saddle.   Even then his rest was only for two
hours.   At 2 a.m. he was in the saddle again, and driving
on the pursuit.   The English horse and foot drove on
right through the night, and the cavalry did not draw
rein till within sight of Louvain, over twenty miles from

[1] All this is splendid open country, grand for cavalry even at the
present day.   From the Tomb of Ottomond, a great circular mound
about 80 feet high, a splendid view of all this part of the battlefield
can be enjoyed.   If Villeroi had thrown back his right flank as suggested on page 109, the Tomb would have made an ideal *point d'appui*
for that flank.

[2] Mr. Churchill considers that Marlborough gave specific orders
for this, though there is no record of them ; but it is possible that
Villeroi would in any event have retreated northwards, as it was the
line on which he had advanced.

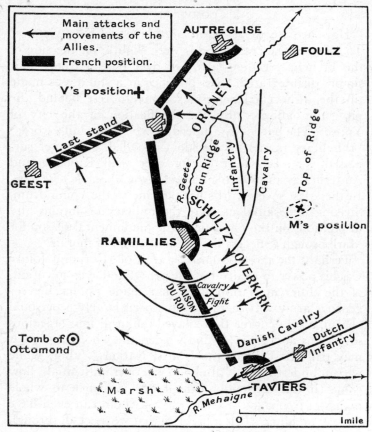

SKETCH MAP 8.—Battle of Ramillies

the battlefield. Five thousand unwounded prisoners and every single French gun were taken; the French army had ceased to exist.[1]

---

[1] *The Pursuit.*—There is not space to describe this memorable operation, which Taylor claims ' constitutes a revolution in military science '. In a few days Brussels had fallen and our troops were well to the west of the capital. Marlborough, like Jehu, ' drove furiously ', but he had his military justification. ' They marched

COMMENTS

How are we to account for this astonishing victory? To all appearances the odds were slightly on the side of the French, yet their army of over 60,000 troops had simply disintegrated. No pretence at a stand was made till the dishevelled remnants came to rest behind the protection afforded by the fortification of the city of Ypres. The battle was, indeed, in Mr. Churchill's words: ' a military masterpiece seldom equalled and never surpassed. . . . It will rank for ever with Rosbach and Austerlitz as an example of *what a general can do with men.*' In these last seven words lies the clue to the conundrum. Striking and skilful as were the military evolutions and dispositions on the battlefield, the fundamental reason for Marlborough's success lies in the domain of morale.

Perhaps the most remarkable trait of ' Corporal John ' was his power to secure the allegiance, and even devotion, of the different nationalities that made up his heterogeneous army. It seems to have been largely a personal charm, a subtle force that allayed the suspicions of jealous sovereigns and generals and welded the whole into what may truly be called ' the United Nations '. But, while we can understand his ability to win over individuals, how comes it that he could extend this influence to whole bodies of troops, only a minority of whom can even have set eyes on him? It is a problem that we meet all through military history. All we can say is that the great commander *does* possess the quality of inspiring this feeling in his men. Naturally, the greater his successes in the field the more this power is enhanced. But what is the start of it? It must be innate in the individual, and to this

six days together without any rest ', he wrote to Harley, the Secretary of State. ' Nothing could excuse the giving them so great a fatigue, especially after a battle, but the necessity of pursuing the enemy.'

extent (but no further) can it be said that the leader is born, not made.

It is to be noted, moreover, that Marlborough's influence was not confined to the troops of his own side. Throughout the battle he possessed the moral initiative; Villeroi was morally and mentally fencing with him, but always one move behind. Marlborough's moral superiority was in evidence even before the battle was joined. As we have seen, the French King was insistent that Villeroi should take the offensive, and the Marshal made great show of alacrity in doing so. But when he got within reach of his formidable opponent quite a different feeling became uppermost in his mind—a defensive instinct which caused him to think more of protecting himself behind a river line awaiting attack, than of going boldly forward to meet the enemy; and this in spite of the fact that he believed his army to be the bigger and stronger of the two. There can be only one explanation of this—it was the prestige of Marlborough's name, a prestige gradually built up in the previous four years' campaigning. Villeroi was, in fact, a beaten man before ever a shot had been fired. It is also worth noting that Prince Eugène, in this alone of all Marlborough's great battles, was not present as his collaborator; the credit was Marlborough's, and his alone.

We are not primarily concerned in this book with the details of battlefield tactics, but no account of the battle of Ramillies would be complete that did not refer to the remarkable ' eye for country ' that the Duke displayed on this occasion. We have mentioned the hollow through which ran a nameless stream. There is no reference to this hollow in any contemporary account of the battle, but it is generally assumed that the lateral movement of cavalry, and later infantry, towards the centre was made by this valley. Hilaire Belloc in one of his books devotes nearly a dozen pages to describing and stressing the significance of this hollow. If one cannot entirely share his positiveness, two things at least are clear. First, that this hollow must have been visible to Marlborough from his original position on the summit of the ridge, and second, that it was not noticed by Villeroi from his battle station near Offus. It must have been clear to Marlborough that this valley afforded a covered approach most (though not quite all) of the way from his right flank to his centre, and in Winston Churchill's view this flank move was undoubtedly part of Marlborough's original design. Moreover, he must have realized that the situation of this hollow would facilitate the execution of the design. Hence, when the Dutch Deputy, Goslinga, was vehemently advocating an initial transference of the cavalry from right to left, the Duke, though keeping his own counsel, fully appreciated that the ground would lend itself to such a move at the appropriate time.

A further note on the *terrain*. The concavity of the French position is a well-known feature of the battle, and the sketch map shows that it was very marked. Thus, the two armies were tactically on exterior and interior lines, and the strong and weak points of these two formations became apparent during the battle. The first and obvious advantage of the *interior line* was that lateral movements could be carried out along shorter lines by the Allies than by the French, and we have seen how Marlborough exploited this advantage. But another feature is that it is more difficult for the commander on exterior lines to co-ordinate and control his forces. The respective battle-stations of the two commanders have been marked on the Sketch Map in order to bring out this point. From his position Marlborough could see practically the whole of his line, whilst an orderly could convey a message to any part of it in a ride of a little more than a mile. But from behind Offus much of the French line appeared in enfilade, and the smoke of battle would soon completely obscure it, whilst an orderly taking a message to Taviers would have to traverse a good three miles. This no doubt explains in some degree the glaring contrast between the almost perfect control possessed and wielded by the one commander, and the almost complete absence of control exhibited by the other.

As a point of fact, there was no occasion for Villeroi to adopt such a concave position. He could take advantage of the valley of the Geete and its marshes (as he did) between Autréglise and Ramillies, but south of that village a better line runs slightly west of south, resting its flank on the marsh leading to the River Mehaigne. The question is, why did not Villeroi adopt this line? The reason may be merely that he had not time to reconnoitre it himself, and maps of the period did not show the accidents of the ground with any accuracy. But the more probable reason is that when the leading troops reached the plateau to the south of Ramillies they found it was so flat-topped that they pushed on forward to get a better view, instead of falling back to the slight ridge in the rear. This is a common occurrence on a battlefield, and constantly leads to trouble, the line becoming too advanced and exposed.

Ramillies is a good battle by which to test the Principles of War in operation.

Maintenance of the objective was the essence of Marlborough's plan. His objective in a tactical sense was the penetration of the hostile centre; on this he kept his mind firmly fixed; no unlooked-for successes on the two wings could drive him from it. We have seen how insistent he was that Orkney should desist in his attack (although it was going well), because it might invalidate his main plan, to which he stuck resolutely right through the battle.

Winston Churchill brings out clearly how the whole battle led up to and hinged on the penetration of the French centre at Ramillies.   Till the village fell the upshot of the battle was in doubt.   Ramillies was the vital point; and no sooner did it fall than the whole French army seemed to realize that ' the game was up ', and a sudden move to the rear spread through the ranks in that strange and almost telepathic way that is a phenomenon of many a battle.   Trevelyan brings out this point better than anyone.   ' Suddenly the French morale collapsed, and a defeat was turned by misconduct into the catastrophe that decided the war.'   He quotes an officer as saying : ' We had not got forty yards on our retreat when the words *sauve qui peut* went through the great part, if not the whole of the army, and put it to confusion.   Then might be seen whole brigades running in disorder.'

Did ever a battle display more clearly the tremendous results that only the cult of *the offensive* can produce ?

Surprise.—In order to mislead his opponent the commander must frequently mislead his friends too.   One of Marlborough's master-touches in the battle was the transference of his cavalry from the right flank to the left. Now, the newly appointed Dutch Deputy, Goslinga, had noisily advised the Duke, when forming his line of battle, to mass the cavalry on his left flank, as the ground on the right was unsuitable for cavalry.   But Marlborough pretended not to heed the advice.   He left a great force of cavalry on his right flank, in full view of the enemy, thereby doubtless deceiving Goslinga, but also Villeroi. At the same time he had to deceive Orkney and his men, for, in order to make a feint attack appear the real thing, the troops taking part in it must be made to believe it is seriously intended.   Thus did Marlborough surprise and mislead his opponent.

Taylor, in his *Wars of Marlborough*, instances another

example of *surprise*, though it is not strictly confined to the battle of Ramillies. After stating quite correctly that ' the determining factor was the moral one ', he goes on to describe the remarkable improvement in morale of the Dutch troops, ' by Marlborough's magic influence. . . . It was expected in the French army that the King's Household Troops would scatter the Dutch cavalry to the winds. But five years of Marlborough's leadership had wrought a change in the hearts of the Dutch troopers. Surprise was one of the secrets of his art, and, of all the surprises that the Duke prepared for the armies and the generals of France, there was none greater than the transformation of the runaways of Neerwinden into disciplined and stubborn squadrons which refused to flinch from the most renowned cavalry in Europe.'

The same phenomenon was observed in the Peninsular War. The Portuguese troops after coming under the influence of our commanders improved in morale and fighting value with remarkable rapidity.

The twin principles of *Concentration* and *Co-operation* are not always easily distinguishable when one is dealing with tactics. Thus, the decisive attack on Ramillies owed its success to the *concentration* of superior force at the decisive point, brought about by the famous flank march of the cavalry. But it may also be regarded in the light of *co-operation*—cavalry, infantry, and artillery co-operating to cause the final breakdown of the defence of the village.

Economy of force is illustrated by the denuding of the unessential portion of the field not only of cavalry, but of infantry. The principle can also be applied in reverse by inducing your opponent to transgress it, as did Marlborough to a conspicuous degree. While he was withdrawing troops from his right, and sending them by a concealed approach to the centre, Villeroi was reinforcing that very flank from his centre. The two opposite movements, of course, enhanced the effect of concentration at which Marlborough was aiming.

As for *mobility*, we see its value in the speedy and timely transference of troops to the decisive point. Infantry, as well as cavalry, were involved, though they were only required to act as a reserve behind the centre. Finally, it was only *mobility* of a high order that enabled the pursuit after the battle to have such a devastating result.

And this brings us to a word on the *pursuit*. As we have remarked in a previous chapter, the number of resolute pursuits after a battle are surprisingly few in military history. For this there must be some good reason. It is no doubt largely due to that *lassitudo certamine*—that fatigue and reaction which supervene at the end of a hard day's fighting. Only the very best troops, animated by the highest morale, manage to overcome this lassitude. Marlborough's men came under this category; which brings us back to our starting point—victory was due to the high pitch of morale and discipline that the great Duke of Marlborough had managed to instil into his men. The battle is truly an example of ' what a general ean do with men '.

CHAPTER TEN

FONTENOY
1745

IN 1739 the War of the Austrian Succession opened, and in 1743 George II defeated the French in the battle of Dettingen. In that victory the King had at his side his twenty-two-year-old son Augustus, Duke of Cumberland. In the following year the Allied commander, General Wade, was so unsuccessful that for the 1745 campaign a search was made for a new commander. Mainly because the Austrian and Dutch contingents would not serve willingly under an Englishman unless he was a Prince of the Blood Royal, the young Duke of Cumberland was appointed to the command with the rank of Captain General. He was given an experienced veteran, General Ligonier, as Chief of Staff to counsel and help him—much as the Black Prince had the services of Chandos in his Poitiers campaign. The commander of the Dutch forces was the Prince of Waldeck, like Cumberland only twenty-four years of age. By contrast the Austrian commander, Marshal Königsegg, was in his seventy-third year.

The French Commander-in-Chief was Marshal Saxe. It is typical of the looseness of nationality in those days that the British Chief of Staff should be a Frenchman, while the French commander should be a Saxon. Maurice de Saxe was a remarkable man, the son of a remarkable father, Augustus II, Elector of Saxony. Not his least title to fame is the fact that he begat 355 children.[1] Saxe had fought under Marlborough at Malplaquet, at the age of twelve; in 1709 he took part in the siege of Tournai, the very town that he was again besieging (but from the opposite camp) when the 1745 campaign opened.

The Allied army was grouped round Brussels when, on 30 April, Saxe opened the siege of Tournai. The Duke of Cumberland, though he had only just joined the army, promptly marched to its help. But he did not do the obvious thing. Sketch Map 9 shows that the direct road from Brussels to Tournai went via Grammont; but Cumberland took the Mons road. The significance of this choice lay in the fact that just beyond Mons was the French fortress of Maubeuge, hence an advance along the Mons road might seem to threaten Maubeuge, rather than Tournai. Cumberland's strategy deceived Saxe, who,

[1] He was known as Augustus the Strong.

thinking that Maubeuge was the Allied objective, sent three battalions from his own army to strengthen it. Thus the young Duke won the first round over his opponent.

At Soignies the Allied army branched off to the west, heading for Tournai. When Saxe heard of this change of direction it was too late to recall the three battalions from Maubeuge. He was, however, comfortably superior in numbers to the Allies, who could only muster 45,000 as against his 76,000. Of these he allotted 18,000 to the investment of Tournai (garrisoned by 7,000 Dutchmen). He allotted another 6,000 to the defence of his bridge-heads over the Scheldt. This left 52,000 with whom to meet and ward off the Allies. A glance at the map will show that there were four approaches to Tournai from the east: the Grammont, the Ath, the Leuze, and the Mons roads. Must he defend all four? Saxe thought he must, and he seems to have reasoned thus: ' Cumberland has made one unexpected turn, therefore he is capable of making another. In other words, he may switch across from the southern road, on which he is slowly and openly advancing, on to one of the other three. Hence it will be only prudent to cover all the roads. Thus I shall be ready for anything.'

He therefore distributed his battalions as follows: on the northern road seven; on the Ath road ten; on the Leuze road sixteen; and between that and the Mons road twenty-four. Between the Mons road and the Scheldt he had no infantry at all, merely a screen of cavalry. Moreover, his whole front extended over seven miles.

But Cumberland, instead of making another turn, was forging straight ahead, making for that very point of the line where there were no infantry to oppose him. This was the situation when, on 9 May, he reached Baugnies, only nine miles south-east of Tournai. Round two also goes to the Englishman.

On the afternoon of the next day, 10 May, Saxe awoke to the danger of the situation, and took hurried steps to meet it. This involved a 'side-slip' of his army from left to right. He now extended his right to the River Scheldt,

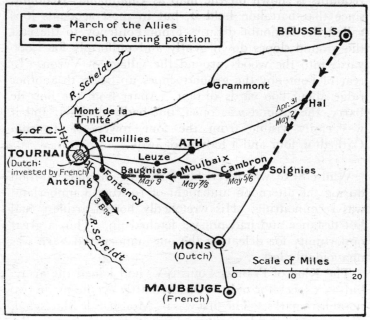

- - - March of the Allies
——— French covering position

BRUSSELS

R. Scheldt

Grammont

Apr. 31 Hal
May 2

Mont de la Trinité

L. of C.

Rumillies

ATH

TOURNAI
(Dutch:
invested by French)

Leuze

Moulbaix

Cambron

Soignies

Baugnies
May 9

May 7/8

May 5/6

Antoing

Fontenoy

3 Bns

R. Scheldt

MONS
(Dutch)

Scale of Miles
0   10   20

MAUBEUGE
(French)

SKETCH MAP 9.—Opening of the Fontenoy Campaign

but he still kept troops on the most northern road, and no less than fourteen battalions to the north of the Leuze road.

But it is only the right-hand end of his position with which we are concerned. Sketch Map 10 shows the French dispositions there. An extraordinary feature will at once catch the eye. It is the sharp right-angled turn that the line took at the village of Fontenoy. From there to the north it ran in a fairly straight line, along a flattish crest, thence along the rear edge of the Bois de Barry, with two redoubts just in front; but to the right of Fontenoy it bent sharp back to the village of Antoing, where it joined the river. The southern of these two redoubts is shown on the map as Chambonas Redoubt, since that battalion held it, but in most accounts it is called the Redoubt d'Eu.[1] From Fontenoy to the east the ground slopes down gently and uniformly for 1,000 yards into the woods around the village of Vezon. In rear of Fontenoy the ground slopes up again to another ridge about 800 yards distant. Apart from the Bois de Barry, the ground was open, but badly drained, and it was easily visible from the four towers of Tournai Cathedral, four and a half miles away.

Whilst Saxe was feverishly fortifying his new position during the afternoon and night of 10 May, Cumberland was reconnoitring. His wretchedly horsed artillery had lost distance and had not yet fetched up. Thus a great opportunity for defeating the out-manoeuvred Saxe was unavoidably lost.

The King of France, Louis XV, had joined the army, but as a spectator only. On the battle eve he made two notable remarks. The first was: ' Monsieur le Maréschal, en vous confiant le commandement de mon armée, j'ai entendu que tout le monde vous y obéisse; je serai le premier à en donner l'example '. The second was: ' Depuis la bataille de Poitiers aucun roi de France n'avait combattu avec son fils, ni remporté depuis St. Louis de victoire signalée sur les Anglais; j'espère être le premier '.[2]

---

[1] There were in fact two Redoubts d'Eu. D'Eu was the regiment, Chambonas was the battalion.

[2] This remark is generally misquoted.

The Allied army moved off at 2 a.m. on 11 May, threading its way slowly through the Vezon woods. At 4 a.m. the Duke of Cumberland rode down the line, and

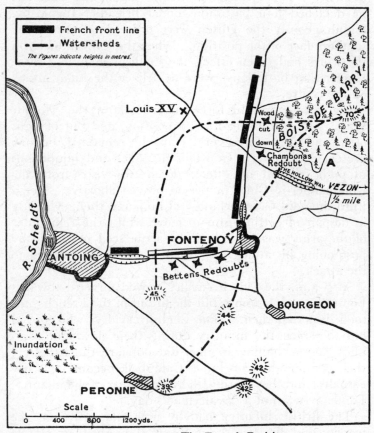

SKETCH MAP 10.—The French Position

learnt for the first time of the existence of the Chambonas Redoubt. This Redoubt bore much the same relation to the rest of the line as did Hougoumont to the British line at Waterloo, each forming a flank bastion in advance of the general line, and Cumberland anticipated Napoleon in dealing with the bastion before the main attack was launched. For this attack on the Chambonas Redoubt he detached four battalions under Brigadier Ingoldsby. Simultaneously the Dutch were ordered to attack the southern face of the position. When these two attacks on the wings had taken effect, the English (including three Hanoverian battalions) were to deliver the main attack on the centre.

Ingoldsby moved his force forward as far as the 'Hollow Way', just below the French position, and out of sight of it, and there for several hours he remained, on one pretext or another. Constant messages and injunctions to push on had no effect. Even two visits from the Commander-in-Chief in person proved abortive. Yet a third time did Cumberland visit him, and then, evidently in despair of getting him to move whilst the remainder of the army was stationary, he acquiesced in Ingoldsby postponing his attack till the main column advanced to the attack.

At 7 a.m. the Dutch cavalry moved forward towards Fontenoy and Antoing, but the fire from the French guns soon dispersed them. The English cavalry, who moved out to screen the infantry during their slow and complicated marshalling in line, did not fare much better; their commander, Sir James Campbell, became an early casualty, and they were withdrawn in rear of the infantry. Fontenoy was not a cavalryman's day.

The British infantry had by now emerged from the woods, and for two hours went through their stately evolutions, ceaselessly harried throughout by the French guns.

Meanwhile, the Dutch made their attack on the left, from Fontenoy to Antoing. But it was a half-hearted

affair, and never looked like getting to grips with the
enemy. In fact, it was defeated solely by gunfire.[1]

Eleven o'clock arrived, the day was half spent, and the
two flank attacks had alike come to a standstill. Cumberland had now to come to a fateful decision: either the
battle must be broken off, or else the British infantry must
be launched to a frontal attack on an unshaken position,
with both flanks in the air, and exposed from the two
advanced bastions formed by the village of Fontenoy and
the Redoubt d'Eu. A fearful responsibility rested upon
the shoulders of the young English commander in this his
first battle. But he did not shrink from it. With superb
faith in his British troops, he placed himself at their head
and gave the order to advance.

The British column, or 'square' as it came to be
known, consisted of twenty battalions, say 13,000 men.
It formed up and moved off in two lines, the three Guards
battalions holding the post of honour on the right of the
first line. But as it advanced, the left of the line overlapped the village of Fontenoy and gradually and instinctively faced to its left; in this manner was formed the
left face of the so-called square, the front face consisting
solely of the three Guards battalions. In just the same
manner the right battalions of the second line, joining up
with Ingoldsby's brigade, faced to their right to oppose
the Chambonas Redoubt. Thus the third face of the
square was formed.[2] (Sketch Map 11.)

[1] Part of this came from the far side of the river Scheldt, thus taking
them in flank. Saxe has been praised for his judgement in placing guns
in that position. But he did not. It was all a happy chance. Some
siege guns were on the way to join the besiegers of Tournai, and, stopping to graze their horses by the roadside, the gunners discovered, to
their astonishment, that a battle was in progress on the far side of the
river. By an admirable exercise of initiative they joined in the fray.
Indeed, this chance intervention may conceivably have been the decid-
ing factor that stopped the Dutch advance, and thus lost us the battle.

[2] This seems to be the solution of a problem that has puzzled all
commentators.

In front of the front line, incredible as it sounds, marched, or rather were dragged, twelve six-pounders; the contractors' drivers had run away with their horses, and the guns had to be manhandled all the way up that long boggy slope—a truly remarkable performance.

The celebrated scene that was enacted when at last the column, harassed throughout by flanking fire from Fontenoy and the Chambonas Redoubt, attained the crest of the ridge, is best and most accurately described by J. H. Skrine in his *Fontenoy*.

On attaining the summit of the ridge, our heroes suddenly found themselves face to face with the French army. On its right, resting on the Redoubt d'Eu, stood the French and Swiss Guards; then came Aubeterre, the line ending with Le Roi, flanked by the batteries of Fontenoy. The improvised glacis held by these picked troops was traversed by a sunken road, which concealed the enemy from view until the assailants were within point-blank range. They were equally startled by the appearance of the guns which preceded our line. Some of their officers pressed forward, shouting, ' Let us take these English cannon ! ' They found themselves confronted by an army at a distance of thirty paces ! We halted instinctively. During this awful pause an incident occurred which infuses a touch of grim humour into the tale of slaughter. The Guards Brigade, on the right of the first line, found themselves opposite the French Household Infantry. Lord Charles Hay, a fiery young officer of the First Guards, stepped to the front of his battalion and saluted with his hat. Then he took out a pocket-flask and ironically drank to their health, shouting: ' We are the English Guards, and we hope you will stand till we come up to you, and not swim the Scheldt as you did the Main at Dettingen ! ' Then, turning to his men, he called for three cheers, which were given with a will. The French officers were dumbfounded by such eccentric proceedings. The Duc de Brion, Count d'Auteroche, and others hurried to the front, returned Lord Charles's salute, and called for counter-cheers, which were very feebly rendered. Then a volley rang out from the French line.[1]

[1] There is no foundation for the famous legend, first put forward by Voltaire, that Hay cried, ' Gentlemen of the French Guards,

Now came the turn of our gallant fellows. A deadly discharge was poured in by the First (Grenadier) and Third (Scots) Guards, and then the Second (Coldstream) Regiment fired while their comrades reloaded. The line regiments in flank took up the tale, while the majors coolly levelled the pieces with their spontoons. Tremendous was the effect of the hail of lead at so close a range. It swept away the entire front rank, killing and wounding 700 officers and men. The other three looked behind them for support, and seeing nothing nearer than the cavalry, which was 600 yards in the rear, they broke and fled in confusion. At this crisis the Third Guards were thrown into momentary disorder by the fearful flanking fire from the Redoubt d'Eu; but Lord Panmure coolly rallied the unbroken companies, and the methodical advance continued. The dense mass scattered all before it like chaff by a sustained musketry-fire. Thus they penetrated 300 yards beyond the flanking batteries, masters of the battlefield.

All was now confusion in the French camp. The King alone maintained his *sang-froid*, and refused to retire. But Marshal Saxe was the incarnation of vigour and activity. A sick man, he was at the outset of the battle carried about in a wicker chair; but when the crisis came he sprang to horse and galloped about the battlefield, struggling valiantly to rally his troops.

A hasty and heated conference was held at the King's battle post at the cross-roads overlooking the battlefield. It was eventually decided not to abandon the fight; a supreme effort was to be made to mount a counter-attack, and Saxe galloped off to give the necessary orders.

Sketch Map 11 depicts the steps taken by Marshal Saxe better than a long verbal description. It will be remembered that the French commander had left fourteen battalions away on the left flank. One-half of these, at Mont de la Trinité, were too distant to intervene in the battle. Not so the famous Regiment Normandie, the

---

fire!' and that the French replied, 'The French Guard never fires first'. In point of fact, they did.

second oldest regiment in the French army. It was stationed just north of the Ath road, and strangely enough Saxe had given it no orders to move on to the battlefield on the morning of the battle. But the Count de Lowendahl, Saxe's energetic second-in-command, galloping towards the field of battle from the extreme left, passed by Normandie, and, on his own initiative, ordered it to follow him to the sound of the guns.[1] Thus when Saxe consulted him about the plan for the counter-attack he was able to announce the impending arrival of four fresh battalions.

A plan was quickly made, and Normandie naturally formed the basis of it. This was to attack the right face of the square, Normandie on the left, with Lowendahl himself in command; next to Normandie came the Irish Brigade, then four guns which were pushed up to point-blank range; then the Carabiniers. All the above troops were simultaneously to attack the right face of the British square, while the Maison du Roi joined in against the front face. Farther to the left various units also joined in when they saw what was happening—on their own initiative, and in a series of unco-ordinated attacks.

The counter-attack opened inauspiciously, for the Carabiniers charged the Irish Brigade, mistaking their uniform for the English. The Irish Brigade does not seem to have fared well in this attack. In any case, the spearhead of the attack was Normandie. We have a detailed and probably truthful account of the regiment's experiences written by one of its officers only three days after the battle.

The order being given, we advanced, and found three of our Irish battalions which were being extremely rough-

---

[1] Lowendahl greatly distinguished himself two years later at the now forgotten action of Halst. See *Journal of Army Historical Research*, Spring 1944, for an article by Mr. C. T. Atkinson on the subject.

handed.[1] At our approach they took fresh heart and charged
with us. We did not manoeuvre, but simply charged with
fixed bayonets, having opposite us six canons loaded with
case, which fired at us point-blank.   In less than four minutes

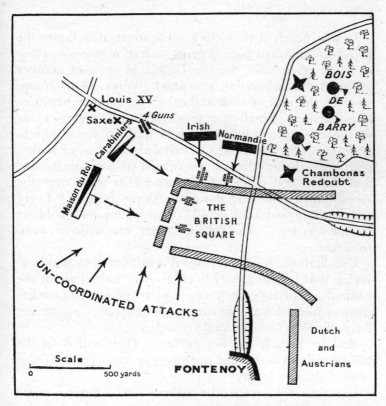

SKETCH MAP 11.—The French Counter-attack

[1] Earlier in the day the Irish Brigade had attacked the British
column, but had been received with such a shattering volley that it
reeled back in confusion. I can find no foundation for the legend
that the Irish Brigade broke the British square and were mainly
responsible for the French victory. Probably the French, with their
motto *Toujours la politesse*, did not care to ruffle the feelings of their
allies by refuting the claim when first made.

we had 14 officers wounded, two captains killed and 250 soldiers killed and wounded. All that did not prevent us from carrying out our manoeuvre. Finally we left the canons behind us, and forced the enemy to disperse their troops who were formed in a square.

It was nearly two o'clock. For over two hours the British column had been at grips with its opponents, alone in a sea of enemies, for the Dutch, in spite of another appeal by Cumberland, remained passive. Our troops were at the end of their tether. The column began to lose cohesion. Finally Cumberland and Königsegg came to the conclusion that there was nothing for it but to retreat. Still preserving a certain amount of order, with heavy hearts the column turned its back on the foe, and slowly and deliberately retraced its steps over the bloodstained crest and down the slopes beyond. Every few yards a battalion would turn about and hold its pursuers at bay. The British soldier was majestic, even in defeat.

Cumberland, having scribbled a brief note to Waldeck, saying that he was falling back on Ath, moved about the column, steadying the troops and regulating the retirement, whilst he sent Ligonier back to arrange a covering force of cavalry and suitable rear-guards.

But the French did not pursue. They halted on the battlefield and proceeded to entrench, fearing a repetition of the attack next day.

Early next morning the Allied army, having made arrangements (including even pay) for the wounded who had to be left behind, slowly decamped, unmolested by the enemy, and that evening took up position at the town of Ath.

The casualties had been heavy; they were about equal on both sides, though the Allies had lost their advanced guns, as the contractors' horses had run away. On the other hand, no colours were lost and very few unwounded prisoners, a remarkable and significant fact.[1]

Thus was fought the most glorious defeat in the annals of the British Army, a battle described by the French historian Pajol as ' without parallel in the annals of war '.

COMMENTS

The battle of Fontenoy is a good illustration of the Principles of War. Perhaps the first point that strikes one is the simplicity and directness of the design, or *objective*, and the unswerving steadfastness with which the Duke of Cumberland attempted to carry it out. Within ten days of taking over his new command at Brussels, and within three days of hearing that a French army was besieging Tournai, Cumberland advanced with his whole army to its relief. Keeping his troops concentrated, he marched forward till he encountered the enemy in his path. He then attacked with all his available strength, and, failing to break through, he marched his army back again. If ever there was a straightforward example of *maintenance of the objective* it was here.

Cumberland has been criticized for the very directness of his attack. Instead of a frontal attack, his critics maintain, he should have turned the French left flank. The criticism is unsound. In the first place, this manoeuvre was just what Saxe had expected and had guarded against. In the second place, the nature of the terrain would have made such an operation slow and difficult. Thick woods filled the space between the Mons and Leuze roads, through which openings would have to be cut. (It took the greater part of a day as it was to cut paths through

---

[1] The Irish Brigade claimed to have taken a pair of colours, but Skrine considers the matter ' not proven ', and the French historian Colin, in a work not available to Skrine, *Les Campaignes du Maréchal Saxe*, quotes the statements of three eye-witnesses that no colours were taken. This seems conclusive.

the woods surrounding Vezon.) By the time the army was drawn up on the Leuze road the French army would be in a position to receive it, and a frontal attack would still have been necessary.

The firmness of purpose with which the youthful commander kept to his design and attacked with his main body although the preliminary operations had not gone according to plan, is also to be admired.

The advantage accruing to the *offensive* is also brought out by this battle. Marshal Saxe, in trying to defend everywhere, could be strong nowhere; consequently, in spite of his superiority in numbers, he was inferior at the decisive point.

Cumberland utilized *surprise*, strategically by approaching the battlefield from an unexpected direction, and tactically by attacking in an unexpected spot. Saxe considered this spot the strongest part of his line; consequently, he did not trouble to throw up another redoubt between Fontenoy and the Bois de Barry. This deliberate attack on the strongest part of the line reminds us of the deliberate attack on the strongest part of the Hindenburg Line in September 1918 and of Montgomery's attack on the strongest part of the German line at Alamein and at Mareth; in each case surprise was thereby attained.

Economy of force implies, as we have seen, correct distribution of all available forces. None should be wasted. None of Cumberland's forces were (unless we include the cavalry, who were, however, frustrated by the nature of the terrain). Saxe, on the other hand, was deprived of the services of no less than ten battalions owing to the faulty placing of seven battalions at Mont de la Trinité, and three in Maubeuge. He was also wasteful in detaching 18,000 troops to contain a town which was garrisoned by only 7,000 spiritless Dutchmen. For all these faults Saxe would have been severely censured had the battle not ultimately gone in his favour, thanks to the intervention of Lowendahl and the misconduct of the Dutch.

As regards *concentration*, we have already seen how Cumberland succeeded in concentrating all available forces at the decisive point (according to Napoleon the supreme mark of a general) whilst his opponent dispersed his.

Marshal Saxe must, however, have full credit for the manner in which, helped by Lowendahl, he attained the *co-operation* and *tactical concentration* of all arms in his decisive counter-attack. Admittedly, the attack against the left face of the square was not specifically ordered by him, but the combination of infantry, cavalry, and artillery against the right face was his handiwork. The absence of co-ordination on the side of the Allies was marked, but this was not due to Cumberland, but to faulty execution on both wings. Had this co-ordination been attained, the French would in all probability have experienced a veritable disaster, with an unfordable river at their backs.

Fontenoy also sheds some light on the virtues of Interior Lines. Although the map does not bring it out very clearly, the French position was potentially one of Interior Lines. The enemy might approach by one or more of four different roads. Now, the space between these roads was wooded in the country over which the Allies would have to manoeuvre, whereas it was for the most part open in the area occupied by the French.[1] Consequently, the Allies would experience great difficulty and slowness in communicating or moving between these roads, whereas the French could side-slip more easily and quickly. This is essentially an attribute of Interior Lines. As we have previously seen, the army on Interior

[1] Clearings in the forest had been intentionally cut by the French.

Lines requires time and space to manoeuvre. The existence of this wooded country gave Saxe the time necessary to make use of them. It conferred superior *mobility* over the enemy—an important Principle of War. Tactically also he was on Interior Lines, but here he had neither time nor space to manoeuvre; thus he was at a disadvantage, and nearly suffered disaster thereby. At the crisis of the battle the village of Fontenoy was in a salient, whose base was only 500 yards. A slight push from either side of this salient, and the whole of it would probably have crumpled up.

The attack took the form of *single penetration*. This, as we have seen in Chapter One, produces a salient, which is in itself a weak formation. But when a second penetration is made, or the attacker is on Exterior Lines (as in this case), a salient is also formed in the enemy's line. At the crisis of the battle the line ran somewhat like this:

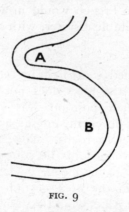

FIG. 9

A being the point of penetration by the British column, and *B* being the village of Fontenoy. Thus *A* and *B* both formed salients; and whereas *A* threatened the left flank of *B*, *B* threatened the left flank of *A*. In such cases the side which has the greater morale will nearly always

win, for it sees the power of its own threat more vividly
than the danger of the theoretically equal and opposite
threat of the enemy's.   Unfortunately for the Allies, the
Dutch failed to make any impression on their side of the
salient; hence, after a period of about two hours, seeing
that there was no danger to be feared from this direction,
the French gradually recovered from their incipient panic
and nerved themselves to join in the great counter-attack
when they saw it developing.

This failure of the Dutch emphasizes the paramount importance of the moral or human factor in war.
On paper, the side wielding Exterior Lines should have
won the battle, but when one half of an army becomes
paralysed, how can its commander take advantage of any
favourable tactical situation?   Principles of War go to
the wall; it is the Strand of *Morale* that is the decisive
factor.   The human factor is also evident in Saxe's
failure to pursue.   It was a glaring example of that
lassitudo certamine of which these pages have already given
several examples.

This brings us to the moral quality of *leadership*.   Here
we can be lavish with praise for both sides.   We have
seen how Saxe triumphed over physical weakness by sheer
strength of will-power.   Not less to be admired is Cumberland's firmness of purpose and cool courage, described by
Lord Wavell as ' robustness '.   Not all were heroes even
on that heroic day; indeed, it happened that a few weeks
after the battle two officers were court-martialled for
cowardice, where the chief witness should have been
the Commander-in-Chief himself, who ordered the court-
martial; surely an unprecedented occurrence!   But the
evidence is unanimous that all through that trying day he
was a tower of strength and confidence, owing to his calm
demeanour and gallant carriage.   *Tel chef telle troupe* is an
old French proverb, and its truth was manifest at Fontenoy.

F

One should not overlook the fact that the Duke was even younger than the Black Prince at Poitiers.[1]

One of the moral qualities that shows its worth in this battle is that of initiative—both positively and negatively. On the positive side we have seen what great results flowed from Lowendahl's initiative in ordering forward the Regiment Normandie. The same applies to the initiative of those units which of their own accord joined in the attack on the left face of the British Square and of the French gunners on the far bank of the Scheldt. On the negative side, a Dutch commander refused to advance at a critical stage of the battle on the grounds that ' he had no orders '. It is a sure sign of a good, well-trained army when all members of it and all units embrace the opportunity of taking the initiative.

A final note concerns the value of *terrain*. In this matter the dice were heavily loaded in favour of the French. The going was heavy, thus slowing up the march of the under-horsed guns, and, since the speed of an army is the speed of its slowest unit, the whole march was a slow one. The wooded nature of the country in front of Tournai conferred a big advantage on the French, as we have seen. Finally, the River Scheldt prevented any attempt at a turning movement round the French right flank. The only way in which the river might have helped the Allies would have been in the event of a French retreat.

---

[1] There are few instances on record where the fickleness of the British public has been more apparent than in its treatment of the reputation of the Duke of Cumberland. After Culloden he was for a time the hero of the nation, the flower Sweet William was named after him, and Handel composed his oratorio ' Judas Maccabaeus ' in his honour. Then came reaction, led by none other than Cumberland's own brother, the Prince of Wales. Egged on by him, the Jacobites employed the Press to rake up any instances of his brutality, and a totally unjustified cartoon entitled ' The Butcher ' gave him the sobriquet by which he is now chiefly remembered.

The ground today is much as it was 200 years ago. The only monument to mark the battlefield is to the memory of the Irish Brigade. The inscription contains an insulting reference to Perfidious Albion. Perhaps the day will come when the peasants of Fontenoy will tear it down with their own hands and erect with the stones one to their true friends—the *rocher à miner*, as a French writer described the immortal British Square; for at present

> Never a story and never a stone
> Tells of the martyrs who die like me,
> Just for the pride of the Old Countree.[1]

CHAPTER ELEVEN

MONTENOTTE
1796

ON 2 March 1796 the youthful Buonaparte (hereinafter called Napoleon) was appointed Commander-in-Chief of the Army of Italy. On the 9th he married Josephine, and two days later he left Paris for the army. On the 27th he reached it and assumed command.

He found his new army—dispersed along the Riviera coast—dispirited, ill-fed, ill-paid, and scattered. He proceeded at once to rectify these failings. He issued a proclamation containing the famous sentence ' I will lead you into the most fertile plains on earth. You will conquer rich provinces and large towns; there you will find honour, glory, and wealth.' He arranged for pay to be raised from the neutral city of Genoa, and he put his commissariat on a sound footing. Then he wrote to the Directorate, assuring them that he was about to carry out

---

[1] *Theology in extremis*, by Sir Alfred Lyall, published in *Lyra Heroica*.

their orders. These orders were to advance on Ceva, force the Piedmontese back on their capital Turin, and then turn east against the Austrians.

His intention was to start operations on 15 April, but Beaulieu, the seventy-one-year-old commander of the Austrian army, anticipated him, by advancing on Voltri on the 10th. At this stage Sketch Map 12 should be carefully studied, in order to avoid a long verbal description of the distribution of the rival armies.[1] The French army was 37,000 strong, and was stretched along the coast with its back to the sea, and with its L. of C. to the west. The Austrians were 35,000 strong, with L. of C. to the north-east. The Piedmontese (or Sardinians), under Colli, were 25,000 strong, with L. of C. to the north. By driving in between his two opponents, Napoleon hoped they would each retire upon divergent lines to their bases.

Simultaneously with his own attack on Voltri, Beaulieu had ordered Argenteau, separated from himself by the mountains,[2] to attack via Montenotte. Napoleon heard of this attack on 11 April, and immediately issued orders to take the offensive. Of his four columns, the left (Serurier) was to demonstrate against the Piedmontese,

---

[1] Very few works on this campaign contain satisfactory maps, chiefly because the detail is obscured by laboured efforts to depict the hill features. As this is primarily a strategical study, I have contented myself with showing only the rivers and the chief watersheds. The reader must imagine the rest, bearing in mind that the Apennines hereabouts average 5,000 feet in height, and that they recede gently on the northern side, allowing of fairly free movement to all except artillery, which must keep to the roads. The maps that I have found most generally useful have been those in that admirable book (to which I am deeply indebted) *The Rise of General Bonaparte,* one of the last and best of the works of Spenser Wilkinson. The maps in most French histories of the campaign are incredibly bad. One of the best accounts—Count Von Wartenburg's *Napoleon as a General*—contains none.

[2] The lie of the mountain ranges and absence of roads hindered Argenteau's concentration, whilst the roads favoured the concentration of the French army.

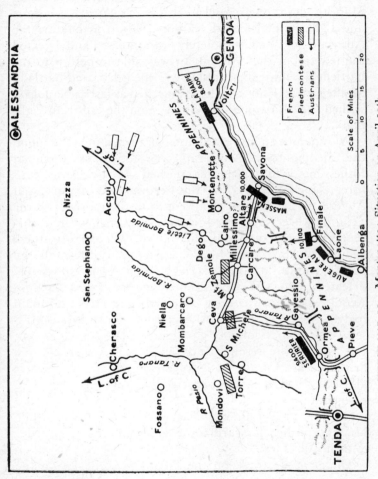

SKETCH MAP 12.—Montenotte: Situation on April 11th

while the other three were to concentrate in the area between the two armies, and attack Argenteau. Sketch Map 13 shows the sequel next day, 12 April. Massena and Laharpe had joined Rampon, who was holding the Austrians, and they completely outnumbered and defeated the few troops that Argenteau was able to get on to the battlefield. This small affair was the celebrated battle of Montenotte. Had Augereau marched as fast as Napoleon wished, he also would have cut in on the Austrian right flank.

Wasting not an instant, Napoleon turned next day upon the Piedmontese. Augereau was to attack them at Millessimo, whilst Serurier pushed on to Ceva, thus threatening Colli's right. But Serurier was dilatory, and Augereau's attack was repulsed. On the morning of the 14th, however, the Piedmontese opposed to him surrendered, and Napoleon once more switched his attack against the Austrians. Massena and Laharpe encountered their advanced troops at Dego, and again completely defeated them. Meanwhile Beaulieu had fallen back on Acqui, where he was busy trying to concentrate his main body. Next day, the 15th, he sprang a surprise on Massena with a small force of 3,000 men. But Napoleon sent Laharpe to the rescue, and finally the Austrians were driven back. On the 16th Augereau had another success at Ceva, though again Serurier was slow and failed to co-operate.

On the 17th Laharpe was recalled to Dego, while Massena pushed forward towards Mombarcaro, in order to turn Colli's left.

The general attack on the Piedmontese began on the 19th, Napoleon now feeling quite happy about his right flank: the Austrians had all withdrawn on Acqui.

During the next three days there was a good deal of fighting; Serurier was now taking his share, and the bulk

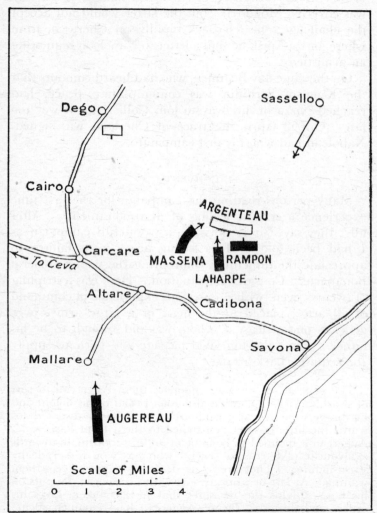

SKETCH MAP 13.—Battle of Montenotte, April 12th

of the French army was concentrated against Colli, who was covering Mondovi. But the latter would not accept the challenge.; he fell back rapidly on Cherasco, from where, on 23 April, he sent a letter to Napoleon requesting an armistice.

On the same day Beaulieu, who had heard rumours that the King of Sardinia was contemplating peace, had reached Nizza on his way to join Colli. But it was too late. On 28 April the truce of Cherasco was signed. Napoleon had won his first campaign.

COMMENTS

Many persons reading this campaign for the first time experience a certain feeling of disappointment. ' After all ', they say, ' it is not such a wonderful campaign as I had been told '. This feeling arises from failure to appreciate the difficulties confronting the young General Bonaparte. Consider the situation. Here was a stripling of twenty-seven, with no previous experience of command of all arms, placed at the head of a large army, over generals one at least of whom was old enough to be his father. The following vivid passage will perhaps supply the requisite background.

The generals of division, amongst them Augereau, a sort of swashbuckler, uncouth and heroic, proud of his height and his bravery, arrive at headquarters very badly disposed towards the little upstart despatched to them from Paris. . . . Augereau is inclined to be insolent and insubordinate towards a favourite of Barras, a general who has won his grade by street fighting. They are received, and Bonaparte keeps them waiting. At last he appears, girt with his sword; he puts on his hat, explains the measures that he has taken, gives his orders and dismisses them. Augereau has remained silent; it is only when he is outside that he regains his self-possession and is able to deliver himself of his customary oaths. He admits with Messena that this little devil of a general has

SKETCH MAP 14.—Situation on April 13th–14th

inspired him with awe; he cannot understand the ascendancy by which from the very first he has felt himself overwhelmed.[1]

But Bonaparte did not only have refractory generals to deal with. The army that he had just taken over was ill-fed, ill-shod, ill-supplied, and under-paid and somewhat mutinous. It was faced by an allied army nearly twice its strength, and it was in a most unfavourable position strategically, should the enemy decide to attack—which he did. That Bonaparte triumphed over these handicaps shows that he was possessed of a remarkable fund of resolution, moral ascendancy, and driving power—in short, personality. Whatever his strategical conceptions, however brilliant they might be, they were worthless unless the driving force of a dominant personality was present to ensure their execution. So we see that the decisive factor in the campaign was *the commander* him-self—Strand number One of our four Strands of War. ' In war ', Napoleon wrote ten years later, evidently thinking of himself, ' men are nothing; it is *a man* who is everything.'

That is one reason why we have selected this out of the many campaigns of the great Master of War for illustra-tion. The second reason is that it is the standard example of the form of strategy that Napoleon is supposed to have made his own—the cult of Interior Lines.

Study Sketch Map 12. Notice how the French army was on a line parallel to its L. of C.; in other words, ' forming front to a flank ', a position which we have already seen to be a vulnerable one. Moreover, this L. of C. was pre-carious, depending mainly on a single bad road betwixt mountain and sea, with the English fleet under Nelson roaming the seas in its rear—a most uncomfortable

---

[1] The historical novel *The Road of Glory*, by F. Britton Austin, also conveys the atmosphere remarkably well. It has been recommended by Lord Wavell.

situation. To add to his difficulties, although Napoleon was making preparations and massing supplies for an offensive, he would not be ready to move till 15 April,

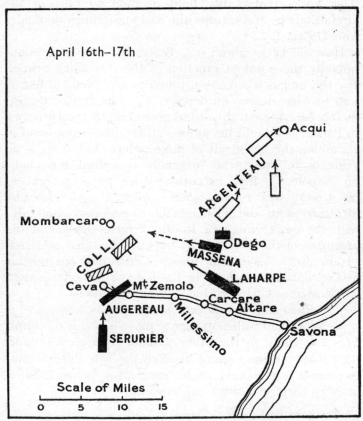

April 16th–17th

Acqui

ARGENTEAU

Mombarcaro

COLLI

Dego

MASSENA

LAHARPE

Ceva   Mt Zemolo

AUGEREAU   Millessimo   Carcare
Altare

SERURIER   Savona

Scale of Miles

0   5   10   15

SKETCH MAP 15.—Situation on April 16th–17th

and the Austrians anticipated him by advancing to the attack on the 10th.

Here at the very outset the youthful commander was afforded an opportunity to show of what metal he was made. He had every excuse to remain on the defensive till his plans were perfected. Instead he formed the instant decision to attack himself, and immediately. This was a remarkably bold decision to take in the circumstances, and stamps him as a masterful commander from the start.

How did he set about it? By concentrating his troops opposite the point of junction of the two allied armies. For this he has received unstinted praise; yet it is uncertain to what degree he deserves it. The fact is, he was merely carrying out the orders given him by the Directory in Paris. No doubt he, among others, had had a hand in compiling the first draft of these orders—but there is no evidence to show who originally conceived the plan.[1] So Napoleon's first executive order as a general to his troops was to *concentrate*. After this he became identified with the Principle of *Concentration*—and also with the employment of Interior Lines—the one is the precursor of the other. ' As for me ', he once declared, ' I am always on interior lines.' Let us now test this his first application of them in the light of the rules which, we decided in Chapter One, govern their use.

(1) ' *There must be sufficient time and space to manoeuvre.*'

Napoleon had sufficient time to move his central column from one flank to the other without interference; and there was sufficient space between the two allied armies to remove any danger of his own army being crushed between them in a single engagement.

[1] The latest book on the campaign, *The Gamble*, by the eminent Italian historian Guglielmo Ferrero (who died during World War II), seeks to denigrate Napoleon on various counts. The first is that the plan which he followed in the campaign was not that in which he had had a hand in 1795, but a fresh one prepared by the new Directory. The Professor has unearthed this plan, and prints it in full. But it differs but slightly from the original plan. In both Ceva was to be the first objective of the army; hence Napoleon carried out both plans in essence.

(2) *The hostile columns must be kept separated.*

By deliberately massing the bulk of his army in the space between the two allied armies, Napoleon observed this rule.

(3) *Only one of these columns should be attacked at a time.*

This rule also was observed by Napoleon. He would not allow Massena to attack at Dego till he was sure of the result of the battle of Millessimo against the Piedmontese.

(4) *Continue this attack until it has been definitely defeated and disposed of for some time.*

This was not done by Napoleon. The Austrians were not really disposed of when on 15 April he turned his attention towards the Piedmontese. On this point there are two observations to be made. In the first place, it was physically impossible at that stage to dispose of the Austrian army completely, for the simple reason that it was not within reach. The force beaten at Dego was only a mere detachment of 4,000 men, the bulk of the Austrian army being at least a dozen miles away. In the second place, this failure to observe our fourth rule nearly landed Napoleon in serious trouble on the eve of his final triumph. The fact has been curiously slurred over by historians. Beaulieu had started his retreat along his L. of C.—that is, towards Milan; but on reaching Acqui he halted, and when he heard, on the 21st, that the King of Sardinia was thinking of making peace, he not only expostulated with that monarch, but started moving towards Colli's army. On the 23rd, five days before the signing of the armistice, his advance-guard was at Nizza, ten miles north-west of Acqui, with outposts at San Stefano, still nearer to the Piedmontese. With the smallest semblance of resolution and drive he could have joined forces with the latter before it was too late. But the mere approach of Augereau's division on the 27th sent him beating a retreat again. Thus did the moral ascendancy that Napoleon had obtained serve to nullify a technically disadvantageous strategical situation. A similar phenomenon occurred at the crossing of the Beresina, during Napoleon's retreat from Russia. Two Russian armies, acting on Exterior Lines, approached the river from north and south, but Napoleon's moral ascendancy unnerved them, and they hesitated and delayed, with fatal results.[1]

(5) *Always attack somewhere.*

This rule was carried out by Napoleon to the letter.

We asserted in Chapter One that decisive results are not to be expected from an offensive unless there are ' ropes ' behind the enemy against which he can be driven. It is a characteristic of Interior Lines that normally there are no such ' ropes '; and in this case there was nothing to prevent either enemy continuing their retreat. Moreover, by failing to observe the fourth rule, Napoleon left the Allied armies free to join up again, a thing that they would probably have done had not the King of Sardinia lost his head. In short, Napoleon owed his victory, not so much to the virtues of his position on interior lines as to the moral ascendancy over the enemy that he obtained by his vigorous and unexpected offensive. It was *the man* who was everything.

It should be observed that, as regards the operations against the Piedmontese, Napoleon did himself make use of Exterior Lines. His main objective, according to his orders, was Ceva. His army approached this place by two converging roads, the main body taking the road Savona–Millessimo–Ceva, while Serurier advanced by the Ormea–Garessio–Ceva road. At the point of junction Serurier should have operated with telling effect; but he did not. One requisite that we have laid down for the

---

[1] A still more remarkable example is the failure of the Federals to cut off Stonewall Jackson in his retreat from Winchester in 1862.

successful use of Exterior Lines, 'resolute and bold sub-ordinate commanders', was lacking. Serurier hesitated, being 'isolated and alone', and the battle of Ceva was won without him.

We remarked above that Napoleon identified himself with the Principle of *Concentration*, and also that con-centration is of the essence of Interior Lines. Now, the object of concentration is to obtain superiority of numbers at the point of contact. Judged by this criterion, Napoleon was supremely successful in this campaign. In each engagement, with one exception, he was greatly superior in numbers to his opponent. The figures are so striking that they deserve tabulating.

ENGAGEMENT	FRENCH	ALLIES
Montenotte	10,000 [1]	4,000
Millessimo	8,000	1,000
Dego	12,000	4,000
Ceva	6,000 [2]	6,000
Mondovi	20,000	12,000

The above table also shows what a small portion of the Austrian army was actually engaged. Some may say that this detracts from the merit of Napoleon's achieve-ment. On the contrary, it adds to it. It was brought about by a more skilful distribution of his troops by Napoleon than by his opponents. 'The art of correct distribution of troops is the great art of war', wrote Napoleon in 1806, very likely thinking of this campaign. Consider his personal actions at Montenotte. During the whole day he did practically nothing; he sat out on a hillside watching a battle from afar. His task had been to bring the troops to the battlefield; it was for the subordinate general to employ them on arrival. At this

[1] If Augereau had kept to his time-table this figure might have been ever greater.
[2] If Serurier had intervened, as Napoleon intended, the French would have had 10,000.

stage the young artilleryman had not in any case the practical experience to manoeuvre infantrymen on the battlefield. No doubt Napoleon also had this campaign in mind when he declared: ' It is always the greater numbers that beat the lesser ', and added: ' When I with inferior forces had a large army before me I concentrated mine rapidly and fell like lightning upon one of the enemy's wings and routed it. Then I took advantage of the confusion which this manoeuvre never failed to pro- duce in the opposing army, to attack it on another point, but always with my whole force. Thus I beat it in detail, and the victory which was the result was always, as you see, the triumph of the larger numbers over the lesser.' [1]

All was due to the correct distribution of troops. How simple it sounds! And yet this correct distribution is, as we have seen, the true application of the Principle of *Economy of Force*.

Napoleon was, in this and in other things, his own best commentator. He was fond of meditating on his first campaign, and it was when speaking of it that he uttered the famous remark: ' There are in Europe many generals, but they see too many things at once. As for me, *I see only one thing—namely, the enemy's main body*. I try to crush it, confident that secondary matters will then settle them- selves.' This has been elevated into the Principle of *Maintenance of the Objective*. In this case his objective was the army of Piedmont; the Austrians were attacked at Montenotte merely in order that the ring might be cleared for the real attack—that against Colli. Napoleon never forgot or overlooked that. With unswerving aim and purpose, he pushed forward resolutely in a steady advance of fifty miles until that objective—the submission of the Piedmontese—had been attained.

[1] This claim of Napoleon's was of course an overstatement.

In all this he showed his faith in the virtues of the *offensive*. ' I agree with Frederick,' he once exclaimed, ' one must always be the first to attack.'

Professor Spenser Wilkinson considers that one of the most praiseworthy features of this campaign was Napoleon's ' unprecedented rapidity of movement, never-resting energy of action '. In this we see the Principle of *Mobility* properly applied. But it is possible to admire this talent and yet give pride of place to moral courage and inflexible will-power, combined with a certain alert elasticity of mind—a flexibility in planning and in re-casting plans that is characteristic of all great com-manders. This he showed when unexpectedly attacked before his own plans were ripe. These plans depended on supplies. Theoretically he could not move till the supply arrangement were completed; *but he did*. He moved four days before they were completed. In this we detect the influence of Guibert, whose *Essay on Tactics* Napoleon is known to have studied.[1] Regarding this matter Guibert wrote:

I will not let my supplies command me. I will make my contractors do double work. The army must live on the resources of the country; it must learn to suffer, to put up with what food it can get, if need be to fast without grumbling. My movement is the main thing, the other arrangements are only accessories and must be made to suit it. The enemy must see me marching when he thinks I am fettered by calculations of subsistence.

This exactly fits the situation on 11 April 1796.

There have been times when our commanders have

[1] The two best books on Napoleon's military education are Colin's *L'Education Militaire de Napoleon* and Spenser Wilkinson, *op. cit.* The chief work studied by Napoleon was *Principes de la Guerre de Montagnes* by M. de Bourcet, and second in importance an account of the campaign by the Marshal de Maillebois in this very neighbour-hood in 1745, written by the Marquis de Pezay. Neither has been translated.

been so obsessed by the importance of building up an all-sufficient supply service before venturing on a military operation that opportunities of hitting the foe while he was unprepared have been thrown away. A study of General Bonaparte's first campaign should prevent the repetition of such a weakness. It is on a par with that spirit of caution—so deeply embedded in our blood—which sees more strongly the advantage to be gained by building up a powerful striking force rather than the advantage of striking before the enemy can do the same. To know where to draw the line is admittedly a difficult problem—one which has not received due recognition in most military treatises. It points to the importance of good intelligence work regarding the enemy. In the absence of this, the tendency is to deny sufficient credit to the enemy for reinforcing or strengthening his position. War is like a set of scales: it is useless to spend time adding to the weights in our own scale if the enemy is adding to his with equal or greater rapidity. It is better to give him too much rather than too little credit in this respect.

CHAPTER TWELVE

SALAMANCA

1812

BOTH the battle of Salamanca itself and the short campaign leading up to it are justly famous in the history of the Peninsular War.[1]

[1] The best known account of this battle is, of course, that by Sir William Napier in his *Peninsular War*. But though it contains many fine passages it is not accurate in all respects. Sir William was with his regiment, the 43rd in the Light Division, during the battle, and he saw but little of the fighting. The two best accounts are those of Fortescue in his *History of the British Army*, Vol. VIII, and of Oman, in his *Peninsular War*, Vol. V.

On 16 July 1812 the British army under Lord Wellington was facing a French army under General Marmont, with the broad river Douro flowing between them, the British being on the south and the French on the north bank. The two armies were about equal in size.

The Allied army was composed as follows:

Infantry
1st (Campbell's) Division
3rd (Pakenham's) Division
4th (Cole's) Division
5th (Leith's) Division
6th (Clinton's) Division
7th (Hope's) Division
Light (C. Alten's) Division
Seven Brigades Portuguese Infantry
Carlos de España's Spanish Division

Cavalry
(Stapleton Cotton)
Le Marchant's Brigade
Anson's Brigade
Alten's Brigade
Bock's Brigade

Divisions averaged 4,000 each. Total 52,000 men, 60 guns.

The French army was composed of:

Infantry
Foy's Division
Clausel's Division
Ferey's Division
Sarrut's Division
Maucune's Division
Brennier's Division
Thomières' Division
Bonnet's Division

Cavalry

Curto's Division

Boyer's Division

Divisions averaged 4,000 each. Total 47,000 men, 72 guns.

The Allied lines of communication ran west, to Rodrigo, and Wellington was dependent on them for food and ammunition. The French lines of communication ran north-east to Valladolid, but the French army was practically independent of them except for ammunition, for it lived on the country, largely by plunder. Moreover, should the line to Valladolid be severed, a new line might be created south-eastwards to Madrid, where was King Joseph with a small army; while still farther to the south, in Andalusia, was another French army under Marshal Soult.

Marmont was expecting reinforcements from Valladolid, and possibly from Madrid. In the meantime he wished to drive back the British army, if he could do it without risking defeat. To effect this he concocted an ingenious plan, reminiscent of (and possibly suggested by) Marlborough's forcing of the lines of Ne Plus Ultra. On 16 July he suddenly moved to his right and crossed the Douro with two divisions at Toro, thus threatening Wellington's strategic flank. Wellington reacted promptly, moving south-west to Castillo, leaving two divisions, the 4th and Light, at Castrejon. (For this and subsequent movements consult Sketch Map 16.)

But while Wellington was thus occupied on the 17th, Marmont was counter-marching with great speed, crossing to the south bank of the Douro at Tordesillas. Thus, he had obtained undisputed possession of the line of the Douro within the first twenty-four hours, and without a shot being fired. Next day, 18 July, he advanced directly towards the Allied army. After a brief skirmish at

Castrejon, Wellington, who had himself dashed forward
to the front, withdrew his two advanced divisions. But
the French, with greater marching powers, overtook them,
marching on a parallel line, but slightly to the north of
them. Thus for several miles on end the curious and
unique spectacle was seen of two hostile armies marching
alongside one another. So close did they get that
eventually they were within earshot of one another.
Napier describes the scene as follows:

Hostile columns of infantry, only half-musket shot from
each other, were marching impetuously towards a common
goal, the officers on each side pointing 'forwards' with their
swords, or touching their caps and waving their hands in
courtesy. . . . At times the loud tones of command to hasten
the march were heard passing from the front to the rear on
both sides, and now and then the rush of French bullets came
sweeping over the columns, whose violent pace was continually
accelerated.

The English won—just; and the whole army drew up
in line behind the river Guarena.

On the 19th, both armies sat looking at one another,
the river Guarena dividing them, till evening. Then
Marmont moved slightly to his left, and Wellington made
a corresponding movement to his right. On the 20th
Marmont started early, marching due south. Wellington
conformed, both armies converging on Castelpino. It
was another race, and again the two armies came within
earshot of each other. Says Napier:

Then commenced a scene similar to that of the 18th but
on a greater scale. The allies, moving in two lines of battle
within musket shot of the French, endeavoured to cross their
march; the guns on both sides exchanged rough salutations
as the accidents of ground favoured their play, and the officers,
like gallant gentlemen who bore no malice and knew no fear,
made their military recognition, while the horsemen on each
side watched with eager eyes for an opening to charge.

But the French were winning the race, and Wellington gradually sheered off to the west, and went into bivouac ten miles north-east of Salamanca. Marmont kept straight on, however, and did not halt till he was in sight of the river Tormes.

The British right flank was still in danger, and early next morning, the 21st, Wellington withdrew to San Cristobal. He was now regretfully resigned to giving up Salamanca and falling back on Rodrigo if Marmont persisted in his encircling movement, for his lines of communication were, as we have seen, absolutely vital to him, whereas Marmont's were not.

But the French commander was seized with irresolution, and for some hours sat still, doing nothing. Then by chance he discovered that the Spanish force that Wellington had posted in Alba to guard the crossing of the river Tormes had fled, and the road was open to the French. Encouraged by this, Marmont continued his advance, crossing the Tormes at Huerta and also farther south. Wellington again conformed, crossing the river by two fords east of Salamanca. That evening the British army occupied a line facing south-east from Arapiles on the right to the river Tormes on the left.

After a terrible night storm, 22 July 1812 dawned with a cloudless sky. Marmont was soon on the heights of Calvarisa eagerly scanning the hostile position. Apart from the 7th Division just north of the village of Arapiles, there was little sign of the British army, and Marmont concluded that it must be continuing its retreat on Rodrigo. After long hesitation he decided to work round to the south, with the intention of turning Wellington's right flank, should he dally on the position. Orders were given out accordingly, and the French army, leaving the cover of the forest, moved south-westwards and then due west.

The ground was open and undulating, not unlike Salisbury Plain. It contained two dominating features in the form of two steep hills, the Northern (or Lesser) and

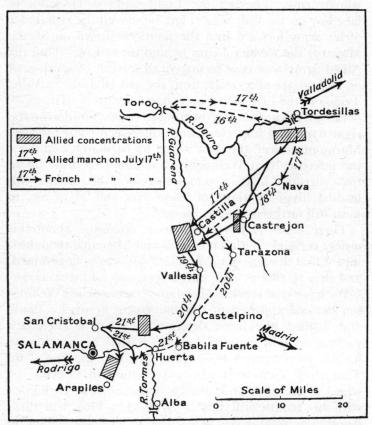

SKETCH MAP 16.—The Salamanca Manoeuvre

Southern (or Greater) Arapile, both rising slightly over 100 feet above the level of the plain. As might be expected, there was a race for these two hills, the French winning the southern, and the English the northern

eminence.   The French were quick to crown their height
with a battery of guns.[1]

Wellington's reply to this threat was to re-group his
whole army.   Leaving the Light and 1st Divisions to
face Foy on the Calvarisa ridge, he moved the remainder
of his army forward into the positions shown on Sketch
Map 17, the cavalry being behind the centre.   Thus the
Allied army was now facing south instead of south-east,
on a great arc of a circle, from the 3rd Division at Aldea
Tejada to the Light Division facing Calvarisa.   The move
of the 3rd Division across the front to its new position on the
right flank had important and unforeseen consequences:
Marmont noticed the dust raised by its march and drew
the inference that Wellington was about to draw off in
that direction.   At 2 p.m., therefore, he ordered his
leading divisions, those of Thomières and Maucune, to
push still farther round to the left.

There seems to have been some confusion about this
order: certainly both Thomières and Maucune thought it
meant that the race of the previous day was to be resumed,
and they started to race, throwing away all precautions.

We have now reached that famous scene when Wellington became apprised of this movement across his flank,
and formed his classic decision to attack.   There are
various versions of it, but all agree that he was having
lunch, when an A.D.C. reported the movement of
Thomières' division to him.   According to Greville, he
seized a telescope, and, after a sharp scrutiny, exclaimed
with his mouth still full: 'By God!   That will do!'
Another account makes him spring to his horse, gallop up
the hill for his look; then, shutting his telescope with a
snap, he rasped: 'At last I have them', and then to
his Spanish A.D.C., 'Mon cher Alva, Marmont est

[1] The slope of the ground was so steep that the guns had to be
dragged up the hill by hand—a remarkable feat.

perdu '. Then he galloped like the wind to the 3rd Division, outdistancing his staff-officers, and going straight up to Pakenham,[1] his brother-in-law, he said briefly: ' Ned, move on with the 3rd Division, take those heights in your front and drive everything before you.' He then turned abruptly, and was gone.

Back in the centre of his line, Lord Wellington gave a series of quick, decisive orders: to the 5th Division to close up to the right of the 4th, to the 7th and 6th to move forward in support of them, to the Portuguese and to Le Marchant's Heavy Cavalry Brigade to form up on the right rear of the 5th, and get ready to attack.

Pakenham's attack came first; it broke like a thunder-clap on the unsuspecting Thomières, whose division was strung out in a line over a mile in length. ' Let them loose! ' shouted Pakenham to his leading brigadier. The brigade instantly charged, ' and the French columns dissolved into a mob of panic-stricken fugitives '.

Next it was the turn of the 5th Division. Wellington deliberately held back this attack until the 3rd Division was well engaged. Then he sent it forward, riding himself between its first and second lines. The result was as decisive as that of the 3rd Division, and Maucune's division was soon reeling to the rear. The 5th Division then swung round to its left, and the Portuguese joined the right of the line. Some of Pakenham's oncoming men also merged into and extended this improvised line, which was preparing to continue the advance, when yet another avalanche was hurled against the much-tried French divisions.

In Fortescue's words:

Presently loud cheering and the trampling of horses was heard to the left rear, and the brigade turned half round,

[1] Pakenham was only temporarily in command, in the absence of Sir Thomas Picton, who had gone home on sick leave.

expecting an attack, when the smoke rolled away and revealed Le Marchant's heavy dragoons advancing at a canter, with Cotton at their head.

Crashing through Maucune's now disordered ranks, they continued their impetuous charge, coming up against the still intact division of Brennier. This also gave way to them, and 'Cotton and his victorious dragoons thundered on, breaking through everything that stood in their way'. Le Marchant was killed, and Cotton eventually drew rein. But the wild charge was taken up by Anson's brigade with equal success. Thus, in less than an hour (Wellington's famous 'forty minutes') the whole of the left wing of the French army was put to rout, and its commander was a casualty.

Yet another attack was delivered farther to the English left, this time by the Portuguese against the South Arapile, with the 4th Division attacking on its right. The Portuguese failed to take the hill, and, falling back, carried the 4th Division along with them. But Wellington speedily rectified the situation with the 6th Division, which not only restored the situation, but drove back Bonnet's division to the shelter of the forest.

In vain did Clausel, who had succeeded to the command, send Sarrut to the support of his left and Ferey to the support of his centre. Both were thrown back in the general advance of the Allies. Wellington strove to add to the effect by throwing in the 1st Division on the left of the Arapiles, but for some reason his order was not carried out.

The whole French army fell back into the forest, where 'infantry, cavalry, artillery, wagons, carts, baggage-mules, and the reserve pack, were all mingled together; the men shouting, swearing, running, beyond all control, everyone looking only to himself—a regular stampede'. There was for the moment no French commander, for

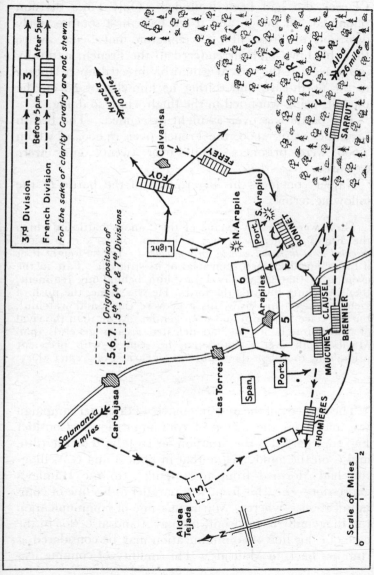

SKETCH MAP 17.—Salamanca—Situation at 5 p.m.

Clausel also had been wounded. Only Foy's division remained still intact, and it fell back in a south-easterly direction towards Alba. Wellington, not being aware that this town had surrendered to the French, naturally supposed that the retreat would be directed upon Huerta to the north-east, and thither he himself pressed on the pursuit, being wounded in the thigh whilst so doing.

The battle was over as night descended. The British casualties were 5,000, the French over 15,000, of whom 7,000 were prisoners, while over twenty guns were captured.

Napier concludes his description of the battle in the following terms:

These were the last events of this famous battle in which the English general, to use a French officer's expression, *defeated forty thousand men in forty minutes!* Yet he fought it as if his genius disdained such trial of its strength. Late in the evening of that great day I saw him behind my regiment, then marching towards the ford. He was alone, the flush of victory was on his brow, his eyes were eager and watchful, but his voice was calm and even gentle. More than the rival of Marlborough, for he had defeated greater generals than Marlborough ever encountered, he seemed with prescient pride, only to accept the victory as an earnest of greater glory.

COMMENTS

The strategy of the opening moves of this brief campaign was based on the factor of communications. Consider Fig. 10, where *A* is the situation on 16 July, *B* on the 18th, and *C* on the 22nd. Note that in both *A* and *C* Wellington had 'formed front to a flank' (to use Hamley's expression)—i.e., his front was parallel to his line of communications—whereas Marmont's line of communication ran diagonally to his front, both at *A* and at *C* (for in the case of *C* his line of communication may be considered as running back to Madrid). This fluidity of communica-

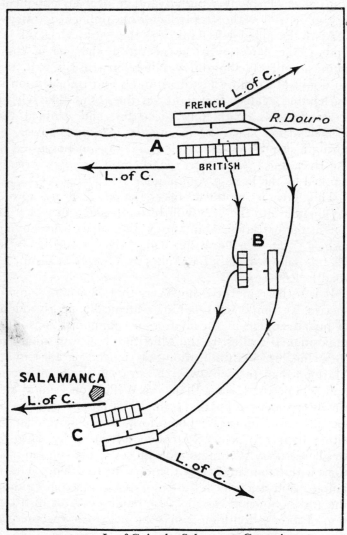

FIG. 10.—L. of C. in the Salamanca Campaign

tions gave Marmont a big advantage over his opponent. It also shows how the supply factor may influence strategy.

At *A* the allied left flank was the 'strategic flank'— that is, the flank lying the nearer to the line of communications. Wellington was therefore sensitive to it, and no doubt Marmont guessed as much and traded upon it by feinting against this flank on the 16th. This clever stratagem was completely successful, and enabled the French army, aided by its greater marching power, to spring a surprise on the Allies, and to gain possession of the river line. Thus were *surprise* and *mobility* correctly applied by the French commander.

This greater mobility of the French army forced Wellington into the very vulnerable position in which he fought the battle of Salamanca. For, apart from having formed front to a flank, he had a river immediately in his rear, and was only four miles in advance of his direct road to Rodrigo.

It is to be remarked, however, that Marmont's initial success, far from benefiting him strategically, deprived him of his advantage in the matter of communications; for in position *B* in Fig. 10 the Allied position was square to their line of communication, no longer parallel to it. Marmont had thrown away the strategical advantage he had held on the Douro, thanks to Wellington's skilful and timely manoeuvre on the 17th. The latter's position at Castillo was admirably chosen for a hostile movement by either flank. Whether Marmont advanced by Toro or by Tordesillas, Wellington could cover his communications with Salamanca, and thence with Rodrigo. This is ample justification for his giving up of so much ground on the 17th. Since *economy of force* implies correct distribution of forces, Wellington may be said to have observed this principle on 17 July.

Thereafter the campaign became a race, the one side trying to get round the other's flank. In this it resembles the manoeuvres of Lee and Grant in the Wilderness Campaign of 1864. Lee earned great kudos for repeatedly side-stepping as Grant struggled to envelop his right wing. Possibly he founded his manoeuvre on a study of this campaign.

Another feature of Wellington's conduct of this campaign is his strict observance of the principle of *concentration*. With the single exception of 17 July he kept his army concentrated throughout. At under an hour's notice he could have brought it all into action.

As regards the exception noted—17 July—the dispersion was more apparent than real. Marmont did attack the dispersed forces, but to no purpose, for they were able to rejoin their comrades. Wellington is personally responsible for this successful outcome. He had taken the precaution to move the 5th Division towards Castrejon early in the morning, and he went over to that place in person, taking with him all the available cavalry, in order to cover the withdrawal.

Marmont also applied the principle of *concentration* until that fatal slip on the morning of the 22nd. Indeed, both commanders showed great skill in their manoeuvres previous to the battle, and the campaign is a fruitful one for military students.

Wellington's marked observance of the principle of *concentration* was quite in the Napoleonic school, and Napoleon must have regarded it with approval, if he ever studied the campaign. (But probably he did not: near the beginning of the battle of Waterloo he remarked, ' Wellington is a bad general '.)

So much for the preliminary movements: now for the battle itself.

It is generally agreed that this was Wellington's most brilliant battle. His conduct of it was, as far as we can see, almost flawless. His sudden pouncing upon his rash opponent, after nearly a week of cautious and patient manoeuvre, has caught the imagination of all students of the battle, and is rightly regarded as its distinguishing feature. Sir Charles Oman in his *Peninsular War* calls it ' an astonishing feat of rapid decision and instantaneous action '. And this is what a French general who had taken part in the battle—General Foy—said:

It raises Lord Wellington almost to the level of Marlborough. Hitherto we had been aware of his prudence, his eye for choosing a position and his skill in utilizing it. At Salamanca he has shown himself a great and able master of manoeuvre. He kept his dispositions concealed for almost the whole day; he waited till we were committed to our movement before he developed his own. He fought in the oblique order . . . it was a battle in the style of Frederick the Great.

This is an allusion to Frederick's oblique manoeuvre at the battle of Leuthen.

Wellington's dynamic energy was never better exemplified than during this battle, from the moment when his hawk-like eye detected Marmont's lapse till the last shot was fired in the growing darkness. As at Waterloo, so here, he visited each critical spot in turn. Indeed, throughout the battle he seems to have given personally the orders for each operation. History does not relate how many horses he got through in the course of the battle. Never again was he to exhibit such ubiquity on the battlefield till he encountered Napoleon in person on the plains of Waterloo.

But there are other points to be studied and admired in Wellington's conduct of this battle. Observe once more his *economy of force* as instanced by the judicious placing of the 4th, 5th, and 6th Divisions in a central position before the battle, whence they could operate expeditiously whatever course events might take. *Economy of force* also involves not wasting any troops. Each division had its own particular rôle, and if the 1st Division did not play a great part, that seems due to the ' stickiness ' of its commander when the opportunity presented itself at the end of the day. Apart from this failure there was fine co-ordination and *co-operation* between the different divisions and the cavalry. The charge of Le Marchant was personally directed by Wellington just at the right time and place to combine with the operation of the 5th and 4th Divisions. The attack by the 5th Division was also carefully timed to co-operate with the Portuguese and the 3rd Division.

As regards the pursuit, it was pure bad luck that it was not more effective. Wellington, not being aware that the Spaniards had quitted Alba, naturally supposed that the retreating French would make for the ford at Huerta by which they had crossed in their advance; instead of which they were able to make the crossing at Alba. Had Alba still been held it is the opinion of Oman that ' a disaster like that of Leipsic must have followed, and the whole of the rear of the Army of Portugal, brought up against the river Tormes, must have surrendered *en masse* '. A French eye-witness describes the retreat as: ' a shapeless mass of soldiery rolling down the road like a torrent '.

Hence everything depended on the pure chance that Wellington had not heard of the abandonment of the bridge. Thus does that incalculable factor Chance play its part on the best-regulated battlefield. The fact that Wellington was slightly wounded at the end of the day—another matter of chance—may have detracted from the vigour of the pursuit, as it afterwards did at the battle of Orthez. It may be considered Chance, but more correctly *friction de guerre*, that influenced the conduct of the battle by the casualties to so many of the higher commanders on both sides. On the other hand, these *frictions* tend to cancel out, and probably did so on this occasion.

G

CHAPTER THIRTEEN

ATLANTA

1864

IN the fourth year of the American Civil War a campaign
was fought in the heart of Georgia that has attracted little
attention, owing to the more important operations that
were taking place between Lee and Grant in Virginia.
This is a pity, for the Atlanta campaign, waged by
Sherman against first J. E. Johnston and then against
J. B. Hood, is replete with lessons for the student of war.

The campaign opened on 5 May 1864, when a Northern
army 110,000 strong under W. T. Sherman, attacked a
Southern army 80,000 strong under J. E. Johnston. By
18 July Sherman had driven Johnston about ninety miles
south and was under ten miles from the town of Atlanta.
On that date Johnston was relieved of his command and
succeeded by Hood.

The Northern corps commanders were Thomas,
McPherson, and Schofield. The Southern corps commanders were Hardee, Cheatham, and Stewart.

Sherman [1] became aware of the supersession of Johnston [2] by Hood on 18 July. As it happened, the new

---

[1] William T. Sherman was one of the most colourful and dominating personalities in the Northern army. He was educated at
West Point, and served in the Mexican War, afterwards retiring
into civil life. He served as a brigadier at the battle of Bull Run in
1861, and afterwards became General Grant's right-hand man in
the West. At this time he was forty-four years of age, tall, angular,
with flashing eyes and rapid speech. Colonel Stone describes him
as ' quick-eyed, ingenious, nervously active in mind and body,
sleeplessly alert on every occasion, with a clear idea of what he wanted
and an unyielding determination to have it '.

[2] ' Joe ' Johnston had served under Lee round Richmond till
wounded. He had, and still has, a high military reputation, but his
conduct of this campaign was cautious rather than inspiring, and
gradually, as the retreat progressed, he began to lose his hold on the
confidence of the army. It was for this reason that he was relieved
of the command.

Southern commander had been in the same class as
McPherson and Schofield at West Point.   Sherman therefore took the sensible step of enquiring from these class-
mates the character of Hood.   From them he learnt of
the bold and even reckless nature of his new opponent.
Knowing also that Johnston had been displaced for failure
to arrest his advance, he naturally expected a more
resolute attitude by Johnston's successor.   This expectation does not, however, appear to have had any effect on
his plan which was then in course of execution—except
to make the movements of his columns more slow and
cautious than they would otherwise have been.

Sherman's plan was to turn Johnston's right, cut the
Decatur railway, and approach Atlanta, his goal, from
the east.   (See Sketch Map 19.)   For the turning movement
he selected, as always, his old Army of the Tennessee.
McPherson's troops were switched rapidly across from
the extreme right to the extreme left.   On attaining
this position McPherson's orders were to make a bold
sweep and cut and destroy the railway seven miles
east of Decatur, then close in on Atlanta along the line
of the railway.   Thomas, on the right, or pivot of the
movement, was to mark time at first, then cross Peach-
Tree Creek [1] and attack Atlanta from the north.   Schofield was to form the centre and a connecting link between
the other two armies.

This plan involved a wide dispersion at the moment
when McPherson reached the railway.   This occurred at
2 p.m. on 18 July.   At that moment he was twelve miles
distant from Thomas in an air line, and considerably more
by road.   But Hood only assumed effective control that
afternoon, and could hardly be expected to take immediate
action.   So the operation went on.   On the 19th the

[1] Peach-Tree Creek runs east and west seven miles north of
Atlanta.

whole Union Army was on the move. Thomas started to cross Peach-Tree Creek, encountering a good deal of opposition. Schofield approached Decatur from the north, while McPherson approached it from the north-east.

On 20 July the move continued. McPherson and Schofield in combination advanced south-west straight towards Atlanta, their advance being vigorously resisted by Wheeler's cavalry. Thomas continued to cross Peach-Tree Creek, and by 4 p.m. had got practically his whole army across.

And then the blow fell. A long line of Confederate infantry dashed forward out of the woods against Thomas, and struck his left flank. At that moment there was a gap of about two miles between his left and Schofield's right. The situation was critical. But before describing the fortunes of the battle we must explain Hood's plan.

This must be prefaced by a description of the man who was now entrusted by the President with the task of defeating the redoubtable Sherman. Among the many notable and remarkable generals whom the Civil War brought into prominence, in some respects the most remarkable of them all was General John B. Hood. Coming of an old Devonshire family, and educated at West Point, he served in the Texas Wars of 1856, where he showed that boldness and dash that afterwards constituted his distinguishing characteristic. Early in the Civil War he became one of Stonewall Jackson's young men, and soon earned rapid promotion. But wounds came too. First at Gaine's Hill, then at Gettysburg one arm was shattered, and at Chickamauga he lost a leg, high up near the joint. Yet even so he continued to serve. Strapped into the saddle, he was able to get about much better than might be expected, though it must have crippled his activities appreciably. But nothing could cripple or tame his

proud spirit. Snow describes him as ' one of those whom
no disasters or physical ailments—not even the partial
dismemberment of his body—nor any amount of external
trouble, annoyance, or ill will can crush '. When appointed to the command of the army he was only thirty-
three years of age, eleven less than Sherman, and twenty-
four less than Johnston.

After this description of the new Commander, the
reader may expect to see some ' sparks ' introduced into
the campaign. He will not be disappointed. Realizing,
directly he had taken over the command, the necessity for
delivering a powerful blow before his enemy closed in on
Atlanta, he ordered an attack to be launched on the
following day, 19 July. But it proved to be too short
notice, and had to be postponed till the 20th. The plan
was for Cheatham's Corps on the right to hold McPherson
and Schofield while Hardee in the centre and Stewart on
the left delivered a combined attack on Thomas whilst in
the act of crossing Peach-Tree Creek. The plan was an
excellent one. Johnston, writing eleven years after the
battle, claims to have been the originator of it; if this be
so, Hood was not generous enough to acknowledge his
debt: in fact, he denies having received the plan from
Johnston. As we have seen, Hood was not able to mount
his attack as soon as he desired, which was unfortunate,
for it would have struck Thomas in the act of crossing
the creek. Further delay was occasioned on the 20th by
the necessity of moving the whole army a short distance
to the right, as McPherson's advance was becoming
threatening. Instead therefore of the attack starting at
1 p.m., it had to be postponed till 4 p.m. The clash,
though unexpected, was fiercely contested by the Union
troops, and Hardee's progress was slow. Successive
attacks were driven back, and eventually, when one
seemed really like succeeding, General Thomas most

opportunely ordered forward some batteries, which managed to take the attackers in enfilade and bring the assault to a standstill. Hardee was about to put in yet another attack when he received an order from Hood to send a division to the help of Cheatham, who was being hard pressed by McPherson. The division sent arrived in the nick of time; but its detachment put any further attack by Hardee out of the question. His troops therefore returned to their own trenches, having suffered very heavy casualties. Hood's first blow had proved a complete failure.

On 21 July McPherson on the left made slight progress, capturing a bare hilltop, only two miles east of Atlanta, and dominating the town.

Patrols were pushing forward all along the line, and on the early morning of the 22nd the exciting intelligence reached Sherman that the enemy had abandoned their position and disappeared. On receipt of this news he issued some orders for pursuit. Sherman's account suppresses the fact, and they are not included in the Official Records, though all three Army Commanders stated that they had received them. Their purport can, however, be gleaned from the following despatch from McPherson to one of his Corps Commanders, timed 6 a.m.: ' The supposition of General Sherman is that the enemy have given up Atlanta, and are retreating in the direction of East Point. . . . He desires and expects a vigorous pursuit.' That evening Sherman's cipher operator wrote to Washington: ' At daylight . . . General Sherman announced the occupation of Atlanta by Schofield, and ordered pursuit by Thomas and McPherson. Vigorous pursuit was made and the enemy found in the fortifications of Atlanta, and not Schofield '! Thomas and Schofield took up the pursuit, and were soon closing in on the city from the north and north-east. But McPherson, who was already in an advanced position, did not immediately move forward, contenting himself by making some minor but important adjustments in his army. He had two corps in line, Logan (XV) on the right, Blair (XVII) on the left; and he placed Dodge (XVI) in rear of them, Fuller's division on the left and Sweeny's on the right. It had now become clear that the enemy still held Atlanta. McPherson accordingly rode over to see Sherman, who was at Howard House, and they discussed the situation together. Suddenly gunfire was heard from the Decatur direction, and McPherson galloped off to see what it could mean. For Decatur was dead in the rear of his army. The sound of battle steadily rose to the southeast, when, in what seemed like a few minutes (in Sherman's own words), ' one of McPherson's staff, with his horse covered with sweat, dashed up to the porch, and reported that General McPherson was either " killed or a prisoner ". . . . I ordered the staff officer to return at once, to find General Logan . . . and to instruct him to drive back this supposed small force, which had evidently got round the XVII Corps behind the blind woods. . . .'

We must now follow the fortunes of this ' supposed small force '. In truth, so far from being a ' small force ', it consisted of no less than one-third of Hood's Army! It was attacking McPherson's left rear, and was threatening to roll up his whole line. Already it had captured numerous guns, colours, and prisoners. It was Hardee's Corps, and Wheeler's cavalry. But how had it got round McPherson's rear in this surprising manner? Only thirty-six hours before, this same corps had suffered a heavy defeat on the northern front of the battle line, yet here it was, apparently approaching from the south-east and striking the extreme southern end of the line! To explain this astonishing situation, we must go back to the Confederate camp on the previous evening.

Here the situation was gloomy in the extreme.

The blow, from which so much had been expected, had proved a ghastly failure, and Sherman was tightening his remorseless grip upon the seemingly doomed city. But Hood believed that the mantle of Stonewall Jackson had descended upon him. He thought of past occasions when the situation had appeared equally desperate but when some bold action had restored matters. In particular he thought of that most risky yet most successful of all Stonewall's operations, the flank march and attack at Chancellorsville. Hood determined to emulate this. Owing to the propinquity of the Chattahoochee [1] on his left, the only flank round which there was room to manoeuvre was the southern flank. This flank therefore was selected. But Hood added a striking feature to the operation that was not present at Chancellorsville—one quite unique in its way. Simultaneously with, or rather immediately prior to delivering his new blow, he staged a retreat by his whole army. This novel stratagem presented three advantages: it would tend to put the enemy off his guard, it would enable Hood to withdraw his striking force out of the line of battle without discovery (because his whole line would be on the move), and thirdly, it would make it the easier for Hardee to get round the hostile flank, because that flank would probably be closing in on Atlanta. Hood's ' battle of Chancellorsville ' was therefore thus mounted.

Under cover of darkness, on the 21st, then, the Confederate Army quietly fell back. But while Stewart's and Cheatham's Corps entrenched and occupied a new line just outside the city, Hardee, accompanied by Wheeler's cavalry, marched straight through the town and out to the south. His orders were to get completely in

---

[1] This river runs from N.E. to S.W., passing six miles to the N.W. of Atlanta.

rear of the Union line, even if this involved going right round to Decatur. A big detour was found necessary, and it was not till fifteen miles had been traversed that Hardee considered himself in the required position. The road he was following headed in a north-easterly direction towards Decatur. Sending the cavalry straight on to Decatur, Hood halted his infantry, rested them, and turned square to his left. This action brought his four divisions in line abreast, facing north-west. (See Sketch Map.) The whole line then advanced straight to its front. So far, fortune had favoured the Confederates. Garrard's cavalry, which might have discovered this move, had been sent east of Decatur to wreak further destruction on the railway. (Such work appears to have been almost an obsession with Sherman.) Hardee had guided his column skilfully, and though he had not got completely in rear of the enemy, he had reached an advantageous position for the attack; indeed, Hood is reported as saying at the time that it was exactly where he wanted him.

The next piece of good fortune fell to the Northerners. It will be remembered that Dodge's Corps had been placed in rear of the other two corps of the army. Thus, the right of Hardee's line, instead of striking the rear of McPherson's entrenchments, found itself confronted by Dodge's intact corps. The latter, after the first moment of surprise, accounted for itself extremely well. A line was rapidly formed, facing the rear, and—another piece of good fortune—two batteries happened to have bivouacked on the bare hill captured by McPherson on the 21st; these batteries were able to engage the oncoming Southerners at short range with great effect. The attack, judging from General Fuller's own account, does not seem to have been pressed with much determination. But it was repeated; and it was during the second attack that McPherson galloped forward unsuspectingly into the front line and was immediately shot dead. This was an irreparable loss to the Northerners, for McPherson was one of their best commanders. Things fared badly for them, also, on the extreme south of their line. Here there was no protection for the front-line troops, and Blair's men were constrained to jump out of their trenches, over the parapet, and engage the enemy from the rear side. Hardee's men met with great success in this quarter, rolling up about 900 yards of trenches and capturing thirteen guns and numerous prisoners. The scene was as remarkable as that at the Bloody Angle at Spottsylvania. 'The flags of two opposing regiments would meet on opposite sides of the same works and would be planted by their respective bearers, in each other's faces. Men were bayoneted across the works.' Hood was watching the progress of the attack from the southern end of Cheatham's line, quietly waiting for the moment to throw Cheatham's corps into the attack from the west. At 3 p.m. he judged that the moment had come. He gave the word, and Cheatham's men were unleashed to the attack, whilst Smith's Georgian militia attacked Schofield's corps farther north. Blair's men, who had just repelled an attack by Hardee, jumped back into their own trenches in order to face the new foe from the orthodox direction. The situation at this moment, if set out in a war game, would result in the director stopping the game and announcing Hood the victor. But the course of battle is unpredictable. In this case, though Cheatham gained considerable success on the left, capturing guns and prisoners, and making an ugly breach in the hostile line, the situation was restored in the nick of time by Sherman himself. Once again it was the artillery that turned the scale. From his position at Howard House he witnessed the setback to the south of him. His quick eye saw what was required, and he immediately called on Schofield for a portion of his artillery. As the guns came up Sherman himself placed them in a position whence they could enfilade Cheatham's men. In a few moments a formidable mass of Schofield's artillery came into action and struck Cheatham's victorious troops in flank with ' a

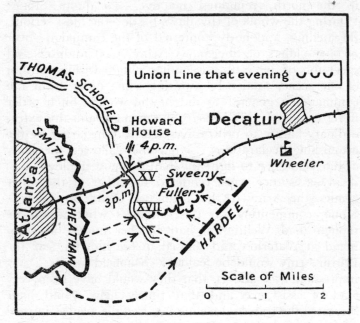

SKETCH MAP 18.—Battle of Atlanta, July 22nd

terrible raking fire '. The attack was checked with ' terrible carnage ' and the Confederates were forced to fall back again. Further attacks merely added to the carnage. The Northerners had now clearly attained the upper hand, and at dusk the attack was called off. Hardee drew back his right flank through 90 degrees, but the remainder of his crops held fast on the line they had won, and entrenched it during the night. The Confederates had captured thirteen guns and nearly 2,000 prisoners, and they had frustrated any attempts at turning their right flank. But they had suffered twice as many casualties as their opponents.

While the battle was raging, Thomas's Army, four miles to the north, remained inactive. To quote Stone: ' During the whole of this day's battle—the most serious, threatening, and hotly contested of the campaign—over 50,000 soldiers of Sherman's Army stood auditors and spectators of the doubtful conflict, almost within gunshot of the scene, anxiously awaiting some order from the commanding general to aid in the work.' Such order never came. In his *Memoirs* Sherman explains this extraordinary failure to utilize five-eighths of his army by the astonishing declaration: ' I purposely allowed the army of the Tennessee to fight this battle almost unaided . . . if any assistance were rendered by either of the other armies, the Army of the Tennessee would be jealous '. Stone, commenting on this, enquires what would be thought had Wellington had Blücher under his command at Waterloo and refused to use him for fear the British Army would be jealous! Schofield asserts: ' My impression was, and is, that they would have been very glad of assistance and that timely help would have increased the fraternal feeling between the armies, instead of creating unworthy jealousy '. He considers that by neglecting to use the other armies Sherman ' lost a great opportunity that day '.

After the battle of Atlanta various changes took place in both armies. Although Logan was the senior general in the Army of the Tennessee, Sherman did not recommend him for the succession to McPherson. Logan was not a regular, which may have influenced Sherman. At any rate, he recommended Howard, and Lincoln approved. This caused Hooker to resign in umbrage. He was the senior Corps Commander, and Howard, serving under him, had been, in his opinion, responsible for the defeat of Chancellorsville. His indignation was therefore natural. In any case, Sherman and Hooker did not hit it off together. All this shows how important a part in war is played by the personal relations of the senior officers. Slocum succeeded Hooker. In the Confederate Army S. D. Lee replaced Cheatham. There were thus three changes in the four principal posts in the Confederate Army in the space of ten days.

To resume the narrative. Sherman, having been foiled on his left, now decided to approach Atlanta by his right. By July 25th the railway bridge over the Chattahoochee was restored, a very fine feat; the Union engineers were a splendid help to Sherman throughout the campaign. On the 27th Howard's Army was transferred once more from one flank to the other. It was just taking up its new position near Ezra Church when, on the 28th, it was again attacked. Hood, taking advantage of his interior lines, suddenly switched Lee across the base of his salient in order to attack Howard's right flank before it had properly settled in. (See Map 19.)

The plan for this attack was almost as ambitious and striking as that of the 22nd. But the procedure was reversed. Stewart's corps was this time to take the enemy in reverse, but instead of opening the proceedings with this manoeuvre, it was to remain in a waiting position on the first day of the battle, and was only to execute its turning movement on the second day. This is quite a novel plan for a battle, and it would have been interesting to see how it prospered. But unfortunately it did not have the chance, for things went so badly with Lee's attack on the first day that Stewart was called to his

support. Even so, the attacks, though repeatedly re-
newed, were beaten off with ease, and with great slaughter,
for Howard's men had just had sufficient time to throw
back their right flank and run up some rough stockades.
But once again it was a case of ' touch and go '. The
attack was held by artillery hastily rushed up, and by
the fire of repeating rifles. Moreover, the Confederate
attacks lacked sting. The fact seems to be that Hood's
weapon had been blunted by the apparently unavailing
losses and exertions of the past few days: the Confederate
infantry would not go ' once more into the breach ' with
the unquestioning confidence and dash that had characterized them of old. It was an almost exact counterpart of
Coldharbour—with the rôles reversed. Nevertheless, the
attack had foiled Howard's flanking movement. The
latter, to do him justice, had expected that Hood would
attack him before he got settled into position, and told
Sherman of his fears, knowing from West Point days what
sort of a tornado he had to deal with. But Sherman
refused to believe that Hood would dare to attack again
so soon after his setbacks on the 20th and 22nd. Hood
took another unorthodox but imaginative step in this
battle. Two corps were engaged in the same operation.
It is an axiom of war that troops so engaged should have a
common commander—an axiom that was seldom observed
in Sherman's Army. Hood therefore placed Hardee,
whose corps was not actively engaged, in command of the
other two. Unfortunately, by the time the change of
command was effected, the crisis of the battle was past.
But the conception was a sound one.

COMMENTS

I hope my readers agree that General Hood provided
the necessary ' sparks ' during these ten days. It would
be difficult to find, in the history of any campaign, a more

dazzling series of blows so rapidly delivered by a retreating and discredited army. The conception of each
was sound—even brilliant. In every case the enemy was
struck either on the move or before he had had time to
throw up adequate defences. In each case there was
little or no warning of the impending blow. In the case

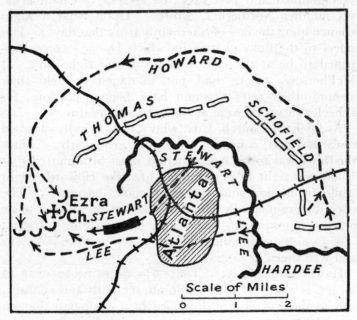

SKETCH MAP 19.—Battle of Ezra Church, July 28th

of the Peach-Tree Creek, Hood was right to strike at the
force nearest to him. To give direct support Schofield
would have had to recross the creek, involving a march of
several miles. General G. W. Smith, who commanded
the Georgia Militia, afterwards wrote: ' If Hood's orders
had been promptly obeyed this attack would probably
have resulted in a staggering blow to Sherman '.

In the case of Atlanta, Hood's blow was bold and brilliant—coming hard on top of a bloody defeat. Hardee's execution of it was also impeccable. General Blair admitted that ' the movement of General Hood was a very bold and brilliant one, and was very near being successful '. General Dodge describes it as ' one of the best planned and best executed attacks '. Chamberlin, yet another Northerner, wrote: ' Upon what a slight chance hung the fate of Sherman's army that day '. This refers to the fluky chance by which Dodge's corps happened to be at the critical point at the right time. If McPherson's troops had not managed to hold their ground, their retreat would have been precarious, for Wheeler's cavalry were at the gates of Decatur.

As for Ezra Church, Cox, who was not kindly disposed towards Hood, concedes, somewhat grudgingly: ' Since the thing was to be again tried, it must be admitted that Hood was right in determining to strike Howard's right while in motion and before it could intrench '. The effective use made by Hood of interior lines is also to be noted. Summarizing the whole, General Smith asserts: ' As an army commander (Hood's) orders were judicious and well timed '.

Hay's comment is: ' That (Hood) came so near to success is a tribute to his indomitable faith and courage, and to the real ability displayed in a campaign that on several occasions put him within reach of victory '.

Why, then, it may be asked, were all three blows so barren in results? There are several reasons, but the chief one may be stated in general thus: *Hood's weapon was becoming steadily blunter, whereas Sherman's was becoming steadily sharper.* The heavy casualties sustained by the Confederates were having their inevitable effect upon the troops, who could no longer be counted upon to attack with their old-time dash and devilry. Added to this,

Hood's plans were hasty and somewhat sketchily worked out. The staff work was bad at headquarters. (When Hood assumed command he spent a long time in ascertaining the position of the other corps. A good staff should have been able to inform him at once.)   Next, the luck was almost all on the other side.   Hood was an ' unlucky general ', and though it seems childish to advance such a reason, and though in the long run luck cancels out, Hood did not have a long run—his run against Sherman was all too short.   In after years controversy arose between Hood and Hardee respecting the battle of Peach-Tree Creek.   Hood said that if his orders had been carried out the battle would have been won, and it is a fact that Hardee extended one and a half miles to his right instead of the half-division front as ordered. The relations between these two were not of the best. Hardee, on being passed over by Hood, had asked to be transferred.   There were also special reasons for the lack of success in the case of 22 July.   The Confederates fought the battle tactically on exterior lines.   In such cases it is always difficult to co-ordinate the attacks.   The result in this case was that Cheatham's attack was launched too late.   It may also be said that the Union troops, both leaders and led, never showed their veteran qualities better than on that trying 22 July.   The coolness and promptitude of Generals Blair, Dodge and Fuller, saved the situation time and again.   At Ezra Church the prescience of General Howard and the speed with which his troops entrenched themselves saved the day.   They remind one of the picture of the Jews, returned from exile, hastily fortifying themselves, with sword in one hand, trowel in the other.

Nevertheless the successive blows delivered by Hood were not so entirely fruitless as appeared on the surface. Their effect upon the political situation was, according to Rhodes, to increase the gloom and despondency that were then spreading over the Union. Sherman's advance had been brought to an abrupt halt just at the moment when he seemed within sight of his goal.

Lastly, Hood employed the principle of *Surprise* in full measure. As a consequence Sherman was completely at sea throughout—a fact that he afterwards tried to cover up.

Of Sherman there is not so much to be said. His wide wheeling operation against Atlanta was well designed to defeat Johnston; but when the Southern command was changed, the Northern plan might also have been. If Sherman had then suddenly reverted to the defensive, and entrenched furiously, Hood would not have had the openings that were presented to him. Sherman has also been criticized for losing an opportunity on 22 July. In spite of his excuse for not using the Armies of the Cumberland and the Ohio on that day—surely the most egregious ever propounded by an army commander—there is evidence that he did contemplate employing them. He was probably put off by gloomy reports from Thomas. If so, he showed the same infirmity of purpose that Johnston had showed at Cassville.[1] He also, no doubt, lived to regret the frittering away of his cavalry beyond Decatur while Hardee was attacking McPherson.

Tribute must, however, be paid to Sherman for his coolness and quick grasp of the situation at the crisis of the battle of Atlanta. His promptness probably saved the day. Cox brings out this trait in his character well: ' He had the rare faculty of being equable under great responsibilities and amid scenes of great excitement. At such times his eccentricities disappeared. . . . His mind seemed never so clear, his confidence never so strong,

---

[1] At Cassville on 19 May Johnston had missed a splendid opportunity to defeat Sherman.

his spirit never so inspiring, and his temper never so amiable as in the crisis of some fierce struggle like that of the day when McPherson fell in front of Atlanta.'

These ten days' fighting afford an interesting study in the interplay of *Interior* and *Exterior Lines*.

Let us consider first how far Hood enjoyed the conditions and applied the methods favourable to the army on Interior Lines.

1. *Time and space to manoeuvre*. When he took over the command, both time and space had become perilously small. Both McPherson and Schofield were pressing round his right flank, and Thomas was closing in on the centre. Hood's only chance was to strike at once, if he was to strike at all with any chance of success. But he was confronted with the difficulty that confronts all commanders who are preparing an offensive—namely, how to assess the right amount of time to devote to preparation. The longer the preparation the stronger the eventual blow, and this consideration prompts delay; but delay may, as here, be fatal, for it may afford the enemy just the time necessary to prepare against the impending attack. In other words, he may strengthen his defensive quicker than we strengthen our offensive.[1] Hood was no doubt optimistic in hoping to turn from a prolonged defensive to a sudden attack in the space of twenty-four hours,[2] but his instinct was a right one. His first attack had the effect of bringing Sherman's flanking movement to a standstill, and thus giving Hood the necessary time and space to mount his attack of two days later.

2. *The hostile columns must be kept separated*. Hood did his best here by attacking at once, but the enemy was already too close to him when he took over the command.

[1] This problem confronted the American commander in an acute form at the Anzio beachhead in 1944.

[2] Napoleon declared this sudden transition to be the most difficult operation of war.

3. *Only one of these columns should be attacked at a time.*
This precept Hood observed absolutely, and he concentrated the maximum force on each occasion—in the
case of Ezra Church nearly half his effectives.

4. *Continue this attack till he has been definitely defeated and
disposed of.* It was here that Hood failed—or rather his
troops failed: it is hard to blame the commander; it
was Strand Two, the troops, the weapon with which he
thrust that was blunted.

5. *Always attack somewhere.* By acting on this maxim,
Hood paralysed his superior opponent, till then victorious
and boasting of marching into Atlanta.

Let us now consider Sherman's application of *Exterior
Lines.*

1. *Possess superior numbers.* This was so.

2. *Good communications.* This was not so. Difficult
marshy ground separated Thomas from the rest of the
army.

3. *Resolute and bold subordinates.* This is where Sherman
failed. The lack of communications no doubt aggravated
matters, but, as we have seen, the force acting on Exterior
Lines cannot expect good communications; hence the
need for bold column commanders. The inactivity of
McPherson on the 21st and of Thomas on the 22nd
nearly landed the Northern army in disaster.

4. *An attack all along the line all the time.* So far from this
being done, no serious attack was made at all. Had
McPherson and Schofield attacked vigorously when
Thomas was attacked, things would have fared badly with
Hood.

Certain Principles of War are well illustrated by this
brief campaign. Hood's adoption of the *Offensive* was
fully justified. Although the immediate results seemed
unfavourable, they had repercussions in the future course

of operations. For Sherman now treated his opponent
with the greatest respect—even timidity. Indeed, on one
occasion he blurted out, ' He (Grant) don't care a damn
for what the enemy does out of his sight, but it scares me
like hell! '   It was owing to this reluctance to take risks
against his brilliant opponent that the latter was not
captured with his whole army a few weeks later. But so
far from that happening, Hood proceeded in masterly
fashion to manoeuvre Sherman back almost to the point
from which he had opened the campaign. Sherman,
who after the war declared, ' You cannot attain great
success in war without taking great risks ', preferred not to
take them against Hood, and as a result he never won a
decisive victory over him.

Sherman also failed to observe the Principle of *Economy
of force* at the battle of Atlanta by frittering away his
cavalry on a distant railway raid, and by wasting the
whole of Thomas's army. His excuse for this does not
ring true, and one may suspect that the failures of Saxe
at Fontenoy, Wellington at Waterloo, and Sherman at
Atlanta to use all their forces may be due to the prosaic
reason that they simply forgot them! In all these cases
the Commander-in-Chief was himself personally involved
in the fighting, and in the heat and stress of the moment
' out of sight ' tends to become ' out of mind '.

Whatever the reason, the resulting absence of *concentration* at the decisive point was a reprehensible weakness in the Northern commander. On the other side, it
is difficult to see how Hood could have applied the
Principle of *Concentration* more thoroughly than he did.
But the rather disturbing fact (from the military
student's point of view) remains that in spite of all the
use made by Hood of the *offensive*, *surprise*, *mobility*, and
concentration, and in spite of his correct application of the
principle of *Interior Lines*, he was tactically defeated in each

case. This is a salutary reminder to the student that there are *four* Strands of War, and that the principles of war and of manoeuvre are embodied in only *one* of them. In this case the Southern army was weaker than its opponent in all the other strands, the troops were not so well armed or supplied, their morale was worse owing to the long retreat they had just gone through, and they were inferior in numbers and resources. In only one respect were they superior—namely, in leadership. *Friction de guerre* also worked against Hood, for he had just been promoted over the head of Hardee, with the resulting jealousy and half-hearted co-operation. It is under the circumstances surprising that the gallant Hood did as well as he did. He was one of the most refreshing and resourceful commanders on either side in the whole of the American Civil War.

CHAPTER FOURTEEN

MEGIDDO

DURING the summer of 1918 the British army in Palestine lay facing the Turco-German army from Jaffa on the sea coast eastwards to the Jordan a few miles north of Jericho, with detachments directly to the east of it, and the Arab army of Feisal and Colonel Lawrence roaming the desert still farther east.

Little actual fighting took place that summer, but General Allenby was steadily forging his plan for the final great offensive.

The first form of the plan was comparatively modest, entailing an advance of a mere twenty miles. But one day early in August Allenby went for a long silent ride, and on his return he strode into his headquarters and

abruptly announced to his Operations Staff that he now
aimed at the destruction of the entire Turkish armies.
To difficulties advanced by his cautious Staff he simply
declined to listen. His mind was made up, his plan
formed, and it remained for the Staff and the Corps Commanders to implement it.

The plan was almost staggering in its boldness, despite
the fact that the British army enjoyed a superiority of over
two to one. The actual numbers were:

British : Commander—	*Turks :* Commander—
General Sir Edmund Allenby.	General Liman von Sanders.
Rifles . . 57,000	Rifles . . 26,000
Sabres . . 12,000	Sabres . . 3,000
Guns . . 540	Guns . . 370

Our army consisted of eight Infantry and four Cavalry
divisions, the Turks of the 7th and 8th Armies west of
the Jordan, and the 4th Army east of the river. These
so-called ' armies ' were of about the size of our divisions.
In the air also we held a decisive superiority.

And now for the plan. The railway from Haifa to
Jerusalem and Egypt (not marked on Sketch Map 20) is
connected to the Hedjaz Railway, which runs south from
Damascus to the east of the Jordan, by a cross line from
El Afule to Deraa, which is forty miles east of the Sea of
Galilee. El Afule and Deraa were thus points of great
strategical importance. Crossings of the Jordan were also
of obvious importance if the intention was to round up
both Turkish armies lying to the west of that river. Of
these, the most important were near Beisan and at Jisr el
Mejamie (where the railway crossed). Thus Allenby had
his eyes fixed upon four vital points. Of these points
Deraa was out of his range—but not of Lawrence's Arabs.
Foreseeing their usefulness in this operation, Allenby had
recently made Lawrence a princely gift of 2,000 riding
camels. Lawrence was also presented with the mission of

destroying the railway at Deraa. How he did so need not come into this account. His own description of the feat is well known.

Of the three remaining vital points, El Afule was to be the first objective, and it was to be captured by the cavalry. While the infantry on the left wing attacked and swung round their line in a great eastwards wheel, the cavalry were to ride at top speed up the Plain of Sharon parallel with the coastline, cross the ridge that bounds the Plain of Esdraelon to the south, and seize El Afule. The second objective was to be Beisan, with subsidiary attacks on Jenin and Nazareth. The final operation would be to seal up the Jordan crossing at Jisr el Mejamie.

The plan was bold and ambitious, even though we had a big overall superiority in numbers, because the conditions were those of trench warfare, and under such conditions a local superiority of at least three to one should be aimed at. Such a local superiority involved an actual inferiority on some parts of the front. But Allenby faced the theoretical risk with equanimity, and imparted his own serene confidence to his subordinates. There is a story that when a cautious battalion commander enquired on what line he should ' consolidate ', Allenby replied airily but decisively: ' On Aleppo '.

The concentration of the troops on the extreme left flank necessarily involved a considerable re-grouping of the forces. Herein lay the elements of danger, for, if the necessary surprise was to be obtained, great secrecy was essential. It is interesting to note the many steps that were taken to ensure this result. The most important of them were as follows: (1) Steps were taken to fore-shadow the removal of G.H.Q. to Jerusalem, on the right flank and far from the impending battle. (2) Rumours were set on foot that there would be a big concentration of

troops in that vicinity. (3) Fresh camps were ostenta-
tiously pitched in the Jordan valley. (4) New bridges
were thrown across the Jordan. (5) Dummy horses,
made of canvas, were left in the old horse-lines when
the cavalry were transferred from the Jordan valley to the
other flank. (6) Infantry were marched down to the
valley by day and brought back by night. (7) Wireless
was kept in operation from Cavalry H.Q. in the Jordan
valley after the cavalry had moved out. (8) The report
was spread that large amounts of forage would shortly
be required in the district east of the Jordan. (9) The
cavalry were marched by night to their rendezvous on the
coast, where they lay hid in orange groves all day long.
(10) The necessary tents had been pitched months
before, and half occupied by the local troops. By these
measures even the local Arabs were unaware of the
sudden increase in the military population in their midst,
and captured intelligence maps showed an actual increase
of troops in the Jordan valley only two days before the
battle.

The Commander-in-Chief himself radiated confidence,
and even promised his cavalry at least 30,000 prisoners.
Nothing equal to this was to be encountered in our army
till General Montgomery promised his army on the eve
of the battle of Alamein, a quarter of a century later, that
they would ' knock Rommel for six out of Africa '.

Thus the plot was conceived and the scene laid for
an operation of which Lord Wavell declares: ' There is
no parallel in military history to so deep an adventure by
a mass of cavalry against a yet unbroken enemy '.

THE BATTLE—19 *September* 1918

At 4.30 a.m. the XXI Corps (Lt.-General Sir E.
Bulfin) advanced to the attack, while the Air Force
started bombing the chief Turkish headquarters. This

bombing was so successful that Liman von Sanders, in his command post at Nazareth, remained in almost complete ignorance of the course of events during the early stages of the battle. The infantry advanced smoothly and rapidly, in a gigantic wheel, and by nightfall had reached Tulkeram on their left, according to plan (Sketch Map 20).

At 7 a.m. the 5th Cavalry Division started on its great ride, moving out along the beach, concealed by the low cliffs. At 9 a.m. the 4th Cavalry Division followed suit, a little farther to the east. The route of both divisions took them close past the battlefield of Arsouf, where Richard Coeur de Lion encountered and outfought the great Saladin in A.D. 1191. Once again on the same spot were Turkish horsemen to go reeling backwards before English cavalry.

But opposition was very slight, and the advance was so rapid that by nightfall both divisions were approaching the long ridge that stretches from Mount Carmel to the Jordan. There are but few passes over this ridge, and the danger was considerable that the enemy would have blocked these passes. That to be followed by the 4th Division is called the Musmus Pass.[1] However, risks must be taken in war, and Lord Wavell observes in this connection: 'All plans in the dubious hazards of war must have such risks; the great commander is he who has both the courage to accept them and the skill to minimize them'.

As a matter of fact, a Turkish battalion had been ordered to block the pass, but it arrived too late to do so, and was

---

[1] The pass of Musmus is not particularly steep, though narrow, and access is possible to the rounded hills on each side; but this would not be easy at night. It is one of the most important and famous places in ancient history, for it is on the direct route from Egypt to Syria, and by it, consequently, Egyptian and Syrian armies used to advance to engage each other.

dispersed by a cavalry charge next morning on the northern side of the pass.

A close examination of the Sketch Map will obviate a long verbal description of the progress of the advance. The leading brigade of the 4th Division missed the entrance to the pass in the dark, but Major-General Barrow (its Commander) fortunately spotted the mistake and switched the second brigade on to the right track. It is an ill-defined, grass-grown track in places, and can be easily missed in the dark. In the early hours of the morning of 20 September the division passed the ancient fort of Megiddo (after which the battle has been named),[1] and at 8 a.m., just twenty-three hours after setting out, it reached its first objective, El Afule.

Meanwhile on its left the 5th Division (Major-General MacAndrew) had been advancing with equal speed. It experienced no difficulty in getting across the ridge, and at earliest light was well into the Plain of Esdraelon. Here it split up into two portions; one crossed the Plain and ascended the steep hill to the town of Nazareth. Here it was hoped to capture Liman von Sanders, but he effected a narrow escape. The other portion continued

[1] Megiddo is shown as El Lejjum on most maps, though there is no village there, only an archaeological settlement. From the great mound which now represents the famous stronghold, a splendid view can be obtained of the whole sweep of the Plain of Esdraelon, from Mount Carmel up to Jezreel, seventeen miles away. Elisha, it will be remembered, covered this distance in record time. No doubt when he ' girded up his cloak ' he spread it out like a sail and the persistent land breeze swept him up the valley. Having myself been bogged in a car along the same road, I am not surprised that Elisha arrived on foot ahead of Ahab's chariot. The *Official History* of the campaign rhapsodizes on the historical memories connected with this spot. And certainly they are striking. Indeed, the fort has given its name to the final battle of the world, Armageddon (Ar-megiddo). Here in ancient times Thotmes III of Egypt routed the Syrians; fighting here Josiah with his Syrian overlords was slain, in a battle with the Egyptians; near here many centuries later Saladin defeated the Crusaders. The memories evoked by the site lead the *Official History* to break out in a poetic quotation!

up the valley and reached El Afule shortly after the 4th Division.

The Australian Mounted Division (Major-General Hodgson) moved off three hours after the 4th, and followed in its tracks as far as Megiddo. Here it branched off sharp to its right, and reached Jenin a few hours later, making a big haul of prisoners in the town. Here it was on the direct line of retreat of the Turkish Eighth Army to Beisan and the Jordan. It therefore sat down and quietly awaited events.

To return to the 4th Division. After a few hours' rest at Afule it continued its march up the valley of the Kishon and down the Valley of Jezreel—valleys replete with historical memories: Elisha running from Mount Carmel to meet Jezebel at Jezreel, Sisera and Jael on the Kishon, and at Mount Tabor, Saul at the cave of Endor and his death at Mount Gilboa, Gideon and his Three Hundred, Naboth and his vineyard, Jehu driving at a gallop down the valley. . . .

But our troops had no time to dwell on such thoughts. The enemy's line of retreat had yet to be blocked, and the division, pushing on at top speed, did not draw rein till Beisan was reached at 4 p.m. The road of escape to the north was now effectually blocked. The 4th Division had covered over seventy miles in thirty-four hours, and only twenty-six horses had foundered—a remarkable performance.

That evening a regiment pushed on to Jisr el Mejamie, where it seized and held the vital railway bridge over the Jordan. The Turkish troops to the west of the Jordan were now in an unenviable posture. The line of retreat for the Eighth Army ran from Tulkeram to Jenin, where, as we have seen, the Australians were sitting astride the route; the line of retreat for the Seventh Army ran from Nablus to Beisan, and Jisr el Mejamie, both of which were

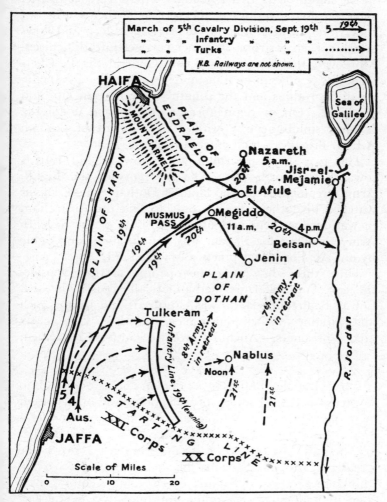

SKETCH MAP 20.—Megiddo

in the hands of the 4th Division.   There were, it is true, some possible crossings of the Jordan farther south, but they were few and difficult.   The river is deep and flows swiftly; even a strong swimmer can get into difficulties. Moreover, the XX Corps (Lieut.-General Sir P. Chet-wode) was now in motion and was rapidly advancing north on Nablus and the country between that city and the river.   On 21 September at about noon it entered Nablus, simultaneously with a detachment of the 5th A.L.H. Brigade, which entered from the west.

The two Turkish armies were now in full retreat towards the north-west.   The survivors of the Eighth Army streamed across the Plain of Dothan (where David watched his father's flocks), only to find the Australians in waiting for them at Jenin.   The bulk of the Seventh Army, heading for Beisan, was caught in a long defile by our Air Force and practically wiped out.

Thus, three days after the opening of the offensive, the two Turkish armies had practically ceased to exist. On 23 September Haifa was captured, and by the 26th all Palestine was in our hands, together with nearly 40,000 prisoners.   Allenby's promise had been redeemed.

COMMENTS

Surveying the battle as a whole, one cannot fail to be struck by the cleanness of conception and of execution that illuminated it.   Seldom has so ambitious an opera-tion gone so strictly ' according to plan '.   The friction of war was almost non-existent, but this reflects the greatest credit on the staffs for their meticulous care in thinking out every detail and every possible contingency, thereby reducing to a minimum the adverse effect of friction.   As we have seen before, and shall see again, it is not possible to remove it or to discount it altogether. To believe that one could do so would be most dangerous.

That is why the prudent commander always has an alternative plan up his sleeve.

The key-notes of the battle, according to Lord Wavell, are *surprise* and *mobility*. The one largely hinged on the other: Allenby used mobility to produce surprise, but he also used other methods to mislead and mystify his opponents—methods described in the preceding pages. One of these methods has not been specifically stated— the foregoing of a preliminary bombardment, which might give warning of the coming attack. In this matter there are two schools of thought; the pendulum swings backwards and forwards. At the battles of the Somme and Third Ypres there were bombardments of several days' duration; at Cambrai there was none. At El Alamein in the Second World War there was one of thirty minutes' duration; at the final battle of Tunis one of about the same duration; at Wadi Akerit there was none. It is a tactical point that we cannot enlarge upon here, but it is a factor that cannot be entirely passed over when considering the principle of *surprise*. Under the term *mobility* we must include boldness and rapidity of decision and action. As Lord Wavell says: ' The soft modern doctrine of " safety first " which so often marks the decline of business, of governments, of armies, of nations, found no place in Allenby's creed '.

Allenby kept his objective ever clear before his eyes —the destruction of the opposing army. No mere geographical objective was allowed to take its place. In the spring a plan of campaign had been drawn up in which a methodical advance up the coast was envisaged, in order to gain possession of the port of Haifa. This was quite sound in its way, but if the hostile army were destroyed, this geographical prize would be almost auto- matically secured. In this case, therefore, Allenby's *maintenance of the objective* is to be commended.

According to the *Official History*, the keynotes of
Allenby's strategy were *surprise* and *concentration*. We
have already dealt with *surprise*. Undoubtedly one of
the chief factors in the success of the operation was the
concentration of superior forces at the decisive point—the
fundamental principle of war. Admittedly this concentration of superior force was facilitated by the fact
that the British enjoyed a numerical superiority at the
outset, but the problem of rendering it still greater at the
decisive point had to be solved, and we have seen how this
was done. To effect it, it was necessary to denude our
defences on the eastern wing to a point where our effectives became fewer than those of the enemy—an excellent
example of the right application of the principle of
economy of force (and also of the advantage of *offensive action*).
But not only was the principle applied in a positive sense,
its negative effect was imposed on the Turks by inducing
them to disperse their own forces, in the way we have
seen.

The pursuit of the defeated and broken enemy is
another brilliant feature of this remarkable campaign.
' Allenby was meticulous in his administrative arrangements before an operation, but in a pursuit like this was
prepared to drive his troops forward on the shortest of
rations,' writes Wavell. And again: ' (In pursuit) he
was prepared to disregard the warnings of his supply
officers, and to call on his troops to live hard and fight
hard, so that the enemy should be given no opportunity
to live and fight again.'

In this Lord Allenby resembled Napoleon in his attitude
to the supply problem that we noted when describing the
latter's Italian campaign. Can we not detect a reflection
of this in Lord Wavell's great campaign in Cyrenaica,
where he drove his troops forward in a relentless pursuit
of some hundreds of miles? Bourcet's notable words,

already quoted in connection with Napoleon, apply exactly here.

The Sketch Map is designed to emphasize the fact that this was from one aspect an operation on *exterior lines*. Though on a much smaller scale, it bears resemblance to Napoleon's Ulm campaign. In each case the lines of advance were taken far beyond the point where direct lines of communication could be maintained. In the ideal operation on exterior lines, such as the Abyssinian campaign of the Second World War, the converging forces automatically covered their L. of C. Not so here. But the risk of having them severed was offset by the speed of the operation. As we have seen, all was practically over in a week. It is to be noted, however, that Haifa fell on 23 September, thus supplying the cavalry with another L. of C. towards the west.

The campaign also affords a good example of the existence of a ' rope ' (in the sense used in Chapter One) behind the army that is being attacked. In this case it was formed by the river Jordan, which is fordable in only a few places, and the current is so swift that even bathing is apt to be dangerous. A few scattered bands did contrive to make their way across, but all military cohesion was lost.

CHAPTER FIFTEEN

THE POLISH CAMPAIGN OF 1939

ON 1 September 1939 the German army crossed the Polish frontier without declaring war. They launched two main offensives at the outset, the one directed to pinch out the ' Corridor ', the other to pinch out the Teschen salient. Each of these offensives consisted of two columns. Those against the ' Corridor ' operated

H

from East Prussia on the east and Pomerania on the west.
Within thirty-six hours mechanized units had obtained
contact with each other across the ' Corridor ', though the
scission was not complete till infantry forces made it good
a few days later.   Even after that, scattered Polish units
broke through from the north from time to time, and it is
significant that the Germans did not trust to the ' Corridor'
as a means of communication at first, but continued to
use the sea.   (Sketch Map 21.)

The Silesian offensive progressed more slowly, in spite
of very thorough preparation by aircraft.   Katowice,
however, fell on 5 September, and Cracow on the 6th.
Tarnow, farther to the east, fell the same day, and the
Government began to withdraw from Warsaw to Lublin.
A mechanized force even penetrated as far as Kielce.
And here it may be interposed that the glaring contrasts
between the German and Polish communiqués, and the
constant flat denials by one or the other, are largely
explained by the fact that a mechanized unit would break
through, and the line again close up behind it;   the
Germans would thus claim that they had, for example,
reached Kielce, while the Poles would declare, equally
truthfully, that they were still resisting several miles to
the south of it.

The third German thrust now began to develop,
striking south from East Prussia towards Warsaw.   At
the same time Polish cavalry made an incursion into
East Prussia, thus threatening the German flank.   At first
this move looked threatening, but it flickered out disappointingly, and thereafter the German thrust gathered
way and reached Pultusk, only thirty-five miles north
of Warsaw, on the 7th.   Hereabouts the German East
Prussian army captured nearly 25,000 prisoners and
126 guns.

Next day, profiting by this victory, mechanized forces

pushed boldly on to Warsaw itself, but were held up at the outskirts of the town, and, having outstripped their supporting infantry, were obliged to fall back.

The next few days brought a slowing-up of the pace of the advance—not surprising under the circumstances—and the Polish Government took advantage of it to fall back still farther to Brest, 110 miles from Warsaw.

But all this time the German thrust from the south was steadily widening, and the southern wing of the enveloping move on Warsaw was developing its pincer-like action. By the 11th advanced units had reached the Vistula, south of the capital, while in the extreme south the Dniester had been reached at Sambor, south-east of Przemysl. This last entailed an exceptionally rapid march, and resistance in this region was only slight; the southern end of the Polish line had been turned, and the invaders were now working east and approaching the oilfields.

But yet another blow was struck against the Poles on this disastrous 11th of the month. The East Prussian army had resumed its advance; its right column reached Modlin (Novo Georgievsk) on the Vistula, twenty miles north-west of Warsaw, while its left column managed to cross the Narew near Lomza. This last success was a decisive one, and enabled a rapid advance to be made southwards across the Bug; advanced elements even penetrated as far as the Warsaw–Brest road. Thus the line of the Vistula was turned, and the only hope remaining for the Polish Armies was a rapid retreat behind the Bug, the final line of defence. After twelve days of warfare the last and biggest of the Polish salients had been almost pinched out.

Now came the turn of the southern army. So rapid was its advance that on 13 September German tanks reached and attacked Lwow (the ancient Lemberg of the

H 2

Great War). This was a clear break through. On the same day mechanized units of the East Prussian army got to within twenty-five miles of Brest, and it became clear that the only real line of resistance left to the Poles was that of the Upper Bug.

Meanwhile, what was happening in the middle of the giant pincers that the Germans had thrown across Poland? It must be remembered that the German advance had been very different from that of any of the Powers in the Great War. Great distances (in one case upwards of sixty miles) separated one invading column from another, and large areas never saw a single German soldier during the course of the fighting. But the Polish elements enclosed within the huge loop or bag, of which Poznan (Posen) was the foot and Warsaw the partially open neck, were cut off alike from information, supplies, ammunition, and transport. Nevertheless, they made a manful, if one-sided, fight of it, and many of them succeeded in fighting their way right back to Warsaw, even taking some prisoners with them. The fighting round Lodz was of an extremely confused nature, the town being taken and retaken at least twice. Exact details of this fighting will probably never be known, but it had no effect upon the ultimate issue of the war. It is possible— even likely—that the remnant of the Polish Army could have maintained itself during the winter protected by the Pinsk marshes, with a neutral Power (Russia) behind it, had not that neutral Power suddenly attacked Poland from the rear. After that, interest in the campaign, from a military point of view, vanishes.

COMMENTS

The Polish campaign of 1939 was essentially one of Exterior Lines *versus* Interior Lines. The classic examples of this in modern times are the Leipsic and the Liao-Yang campaigns. Let us start with a brief reference to the Leipsic campaign of 1813, and see what resemblance it has to the campaign in Poland.

SKETCH MAP 21.—Invasion of Poland, 1939

In the autumn of 1813 Napoleon found himself with an army of 350,000 men opposed by three Allied armies: 320,000 under Schwartzenberg to the south, 95,000 under Blücher to the east, and 110,000 under Bernadotte to the north.   Napoleon turned first upon Schwartzenberg, and defeated him at Dresden, but did not trouble to pursue. Meanwhile Blücher was approaching from the east. Napoleon thereupon turned upon this new antagonist, but Blücher merely fell back before him.   Schwartzenberg took advantage of the respite to advance again.   Whereupon the Emperor returned to Dresden.   Blücher, in turn, took advantage of the respite to push north-east towards Bernadotte.   Meanwhile Napoleon remained irresolutely at Dresden.   All three Allied armies now converged towards Leipsic, to the west of Dresden.   Napoleon could not afford to allow them to unite on his line of retreat, so he moved to Leipsic himself.   Here the three Allied armies converged on him and defeated him decisively in the Battle of the Nations.

This campaign has, of course, been studied by numerous commentators.   Count von Wartenburg is one of the best known of them.   He first examines whether Napoleon was justified (for the first time in his life) in trusting to a great defensive plan.   Napoleon had written to Ney at the outset : ' It seems to me that to bring about a decisive and brilliant result the best way is to keep in a close formation and allow the enemy to approach '.   This he did, with the disastrous results that we know.   Kuropatkin pursued the same plan at Liao-Yang, with almost equally disastrous results.   Was Napoleon, then, justified in resorting to the defensive?   Wartenburg gives as his opinion : ' He was only right if circumstances compelled him to do it, for without being absolutely forced to it no great leader will renounce the offensive—the more effective form of warfare '.   He, however, comes to the conclusion that the Emperor was forced to it, and proceeds to give his idea of how this defensive should be carried out.   ' The most effective form of defence consists always in short offensive dashes against that one of the concentrically approaching enemies who is most easily reached and threatens to become the most dangerous.' But this is just what Napoleon did—at the outset.   Let us turn to another and, in my opinion, profounder critic, the Frenchman Colonel A. Grouard, who in 1897 wrote a remarkable book entitled *La campagne de 1813 et les lignes intérieures*.   (Unfortunately, it has never been translated into English.)   One of the main conditions that the author gives for the success of interior lines is that a general so placed must select one of his opponents to attack and must not desist till he has rendered that opponent incapable of resuming the offensive as soon as his back is turned.   This is exactly the mistake that Napoleon made, first against Schwartzenberg and next against Blücher.   Moreover, in the last phase of the campaign he no longer had the requisite time and space to manoeuvre.

Let us now consider what bearing all this has on the Polish campaign.   First of all, were the Poles (who held the interior lines) justified in resorting to the strategic defensive? Undoubtedly they were;   they had no option in the matter.   Hence it follows that their only hope of success, by the analogy of the Leipsic and Liao-Yang campaigns, was to strike one or other of their converging opponents hard while there was yet time and space to do so.   Failing that, a rapid retreat out of the salient was indicated—in other words, to the line of the Vistula through Warsaw, or to the Bug through Brest. A converging attack on East Prussia offered the only possible chance of success.

Let us now consider the situation from the German side, reversing the reasoning process.   The condition for their success, on the same analogy, was to advance so rapidly with their converging armies as to deny the requisite time and space to their opponents.   This is precisely what they did.   Now, there are two ways of denying your opponent this requisite time and space. One is by advancing rapidly yourself; the other is by preventing your opponent moving rapidly. The Germans achieved the first by means of their mechanized units, and by the good marching powers of their infantry; they achieved the second by blinding the enemy—thanks to their own air supremacy—and by paralysing him by bombing his railways, roads, and bridges. Thus the only real chance the Poles had of striking a blow rapidly was by means of their cavalry. These were of magnificent quality, but they were as much use against masses of unbroken tanks as Don Quixote's lance was against the windmill.

It follows, then, that unless the Poles could beat a rapid retreat to the line of the Vistula or the Bug, they would, by reason of their interior lines, meet with a crushing defeat. There is reason to suppose that a rapid retreat to one of these lines was part of their original plan. But the suddenness of the German attack, its rapidity, and the paralysing effect of the German aircraft caused this plan to collapse. The result was that the Germans were able to play their favourite game of double envelopment time and again during the brief campaign. This, in conjunction with surprise and mobility, was successful on each occasion.

The shape of the frontier lent itself admirably to this process. There were no less than three Polish salients that could be immediately 'snuffed out' unless the Poles had the time and opportunity to counter-attack, which, as we have seen, they had not. The first and most obvious one was the so-called Corridor. It was only fifty miles across; hence two forces advancing from either side would only have twenty-five miles to traverse. Secondly, there was the Silesian salient, of which Cracow was the centre and Teschen the apex. Thirdly, there was the huge salient between East Prussia and Silesia, of which Warsaw was the centre and Poznan (Posen) the apex.

The Germans for a generation had been brought up on the theory of 'double envelopment'. General von Schlieffen had popularized it when he published his famous study of the Battle of Cannae, the classic instance of double envelopment. The German plan of 1914 was founded on it, and they frequently applied it in the course of the war, notably at Cambrai in 1917, where we had created a pronounced salient. The German counter-attack was directed against the two sides of the salient, while the apex was not attacked at all. Similarly, on 21 March the German attack fell solely upon its two flanks, but before the salient could be pinched out we abandoned it. The Polish frontier thus formed a line admirably adapted for the German favourite tactics. All that was required was a denial to the Poles of time and space to manoeuvre. This was ensured by a variety of measures. First, the Air Force. At the crack of dawn on 1 September, German bombers penetrated the un-suspecting and sleeping country, and delivered a series of devastating attacks against Polish aerodromes with con-spicuous success. According to some accounts upwards of half the Polish aircraft were thus put out of action on the first morning of the war. We heard, at the time, of the comparatively spasmodic attacks on Warsaw, but the much more important attacks on the aerodromes went unrecorded.[1]

Thus the Poles were blinded—the first requisite. The second requisite was rapid movement by the German invading forces. This was ensured by the bold use of mechanized forces in the vanguard. Since these forces would outstrip their supporting infantry, thus rendering

[1] The sudden attack by Germany before declaring war was a great handicap to the Poles.

their flanks particularly vulnerable, they were accompanied by aeroplanes, which bombed and machine-gunned, and thus protected those flanks.

The third requisite was to delay the advance of Polish reinforcements to the threatened points. This was ensured by the destruction from the air of roads, railways, bridges, and culverts by which the reinforcements would have to pass.

The fourth requisite was that the inception of the moves of these reinforcements should be delayed by harrying the headquarters that initiated them. This was achieved by bombing the headquarter staffs. Owing to their admirable espionage system, the Germans were able to trace every move of Marshal Smigly-Rydz, and to harry him from pillar to post. It is even claimed that moves of his headquarters were broadcast on the Russian wireless within two hours of their taking place.

The Poles, on the other hand, were deficient in mechanized transport; they depended largely on their magnificent and numerous cavalry. Unfortunately, the nature of the country and the dryness of the ground favoured the German mechanized and armoured vehicles, and cavalry simply could not compete. They had a few local cavalry successes, but these were too spasmodic to affect the issue.

A further handicap to the Poles was that the richest and most industrial part of their country was close to the German frontier—Polish Silesia. It is true that steps were being taken to transfer many Polish industries to a less vulnerable region to the east of the Vistula; but this was only in course of execution, and the temptation to hold on to the industrial triangle, Cracow–Katowice–Teschen, resulted in large forces being stationed farther forward than was prudent, well within the second salient to which we have referred.

Moreover, the Germans had the advantage of being able to marshal their forces to their liking all along the frontier at their leisure. Owing to their virtual control of Slovakia, they were able to turn the original line of Polish defences and strike up northwards towards Cracow, across those same Carpathians that had witnessed a protracted struggle between them and the Russians in 1915. It is usually supposed that the Carpathian passes are few in number. Study of a large-scale map disproves this. Indeed, from the Jablonika Pass to the Dukla (familiar names in 1915) there are no less than fourteen first-class roads crossing the frontier on a frontage of 110 miles; that is to say, on an average one good road to every eight miles of frontier. In addition, there were many second-grade roads. It seemed clear, according to those who studied the map before the outbreak of the war, that a dangerous attack would probably be launched northwards from Slovakia.

Finally, the Poles were necessarily on the defensive, and in this case the fundamental disadvantage of the defensive was manifest, for the defender had an immense frontier to hold; he could not afford to neglect any of it entirely, and therefore he had not sufficient troops to be in strength anywhere. The attacker, on the other hand, could neglect certain sections entirely, and concentrate his strength where he wanted it.

All the elements, including the sun, had fought for Germany. Surprise, air power, espionage, mechanization in a favourable terrain, and weight of metal had been on the side of the big battalions. Moreover, the Germans were presented with that inestimable boon—exterior lines—in circumstances which denied to their opponents suitable opportunity to manoeuvre. All the factors favouring the application of exterior lines were in their favour—superior numbers, good communications, bold

H 2*

and resolute commanders. Finally, owing to the con-
figuration of the frontier, they were able to threaten their
opponents' L. of C. without endangering their own.

When we consider all the above factors, we cannot fail
to perceive how hopelessly the scales were weighted
against unfortunate Poland from the outset, and we
realize that it would require little short of a miracle to
save her from rapid military defeat. Her only possible
allies—Generals Mud and Rain—failed her, and, left to
her fate, the outcome, despite the magnificent bravery
and sacrifice of her troops, was inevitable.

CHAPTER SIXTEEN

THE TUNISIAN CAMPAIGN, 1943

THIS remarkable campaign opens with the landing in
North Africa on 8 November 1942 of the nucleus of an
Anglo-American army. Owing to the fact that the
U.S.A. were on terms with Vichy France, whereas the
U.K. was not, the force was given a predominantly
American complexion, with an American commander.
In actual numbers the greater part of the force was
British—six battalions with complementary troops, as
against three battalions. Moreover, the bulk of the
Americans landed at Casablanca and went into training,
whereas the British, who landed three battalions at Oran
and three near Algiers, advanced to meet the Germans.
Political considerations had largely inspired the expedition
and its peculiar composition at the outset. It was hoped
to bring over the considerable French army in North
Africa to the Allied cause, as a preliminary to an attack
on Italy.

It was estimated that the liquidation of Morocco and

Algeria would take about four weeks. That accomplished, the army would advance eastwards to join forces with the Eighth Army, which at the moment of landing was advancing west abreast of Sidi Barrani.

The two armies were no less than 1,300 miles apart in a straight line, and not far short of 2,000 miles by road. The plan was therefore immense both in scope and ambition, and it may be noted that from conception to full fruition was a period of exactly twelve months.

It was calculated that the two armies would join up near Tripoli, which was about equi-distant from both armies. But the unexpectedly rapid advance of the Eighth Army necessarily modified this plan; at the end of four weeks, when the First Army (as we will in future call it) was timed to commence its advance, the Eighth Army had entered Tripolitania.

Another unexpected fact caused an alteration of the plan—the resistance of the Vichy French in Algeria was so speedily overcome that the British contingent was left for the time being without a specific task. It was therefore decided to make a dash for Tunisia. Although the Germans could land in the country by air long before our troops could get there by land, it was hoped that the local French troops would offer sufficient opposition to make the project feasible.

The attempt was admittedly a gamble, but it nearly came off. Two tiny columns made the attempt, each of three battalions together with a few guns and tanks. The northern column advanced on Bizerta, via Beja, the southern, on a parallel road twenty miles farther south, on Tunis via Medjez el Bab. It was near this latter place that the first serious contact with the enemy was obtained, on 24 November. Driving the Germans before it, the southern column reached Tebourba on the 27th, expecting to get contact with the northern column down the road from Mateur (see Sketch Map 22). But instead of British, German tanks appeared from that direction, and after a gallant action in which the artillery greatly distinguished itself, the force was obliged to fall back to Medjez el Bab. Here it dug in, and the line was carried northwards by the northern column, which had also had to fall back from near Mateur. Both columns had penetrated within twenty miles of their respective objectives, but chance and *friction de guerre* were against them. In the first place, the winter rains came unexpectedly early and heavily, and made the construction of advanced landing-grounds difficult; consequently our troops had little air support. In the second place, the French authorities in Tunisia were either weak or treacherous, and gave up their landing-grounds to the Germans, who were thus able to land ground troops in large numbers and give them fighter protection. The result was that the British troops were outnumbered by two to one, and were only able to maintain their ground with difficulty.

Meanwhile the Eighth Army had reached Tripolitania, fresh divisions were gradually arriving in Algeria, and the U.S.A. troops, having completed their training in Morocco, were coming up to the front.

The line was gradually extended to the south as reinforcements rolled in for both sides. By the beginning of February 1943 the Americans held the southern end of the line, reaching to the vicinity of Gafsa, thirty miles north of the extensive salt lakes lying westwards of Gabes. By this time the advanced-guard of the Eighth Army had come up against the Mareth Line some sixty miles to the southeast of the lakes. The inland flanks of the two armies lay in the desert, which was empty except for the few wandering bands of Fighting French. But once the Mareth Line was breached, the Allied Armies would be within a few days' march of one another. The situation was assuming an interesting strategical aspect.

Marshal Rommel had retreated with the remnants of his Africa Corps, carefully avoiding serious contact with his pursuers until he was safely, as he thought, behind the Mareth Line. The kernel of his army consisted of the 15th and the 21st Panzer Divisions, which had been carefully nursed during the course of the long retreat and had had most of their losses made up. Rommel was therefore in possession of a powerful striking-force at the beginning of February. Moreover, as he retreated he fell in with the dumps and depots of ammunition and supplies, whereas the Eighth Army had to bring its supplies with it, apart from an uncertain amount that could be conveyed by sea.[1] Consequently, during the greater part of February only the 7th Armoured Division stood facing the Mareth Line. Rommel thus found himself between two hostile forces, one consisting of a single armoured division, and the other of fresh, untried American troops. Moreover, between these two forces lay the great salt lakes and the formidable Mareth Line. Rommel sat in the middle with a highly mobile and veteran force. Thus was offered as favourable an opportunity to exploit a position on *interior lines* as can well be conceived. And Rommel proceeded to exploit it.

Two objectives lay before him: one immediate and the other ultimate. The immediate objective was the continued separation of the two hostile forces; the ultimate objective was to destroy either or both of them before the other could come to the assistance of its fellow. In view of the fact that the Eighth Army had the longer lines of communication, and could less easily be reinforced or supported, it formed the most favourable objective

---

[1] In addition a storm in Benghazi harbour in December sank many of our supply ships, thus disorganizing the supply system.

against which to launch the main attack: hence the American corps was indicated as Rommel's immediate, and the Eighth Army his ultimate objective. Sketch Map 22 shows with a minimum expenditure of words how he set about it and what measure of success he attained.

Leaving a garrison, mainly of Italian troops, in the Mareth Line, he dashed with his two Panzer Divisions northwards for a hundred miles and then north-westwards for another fifty miles, and attacked the Americans in the direction of Tebessa on 14 February. The attack was unexpected and completely successful; by the 21st it had penetrated within a few miles of Thala and Tebessa, the latter an essential road and railway junction, besides being the advanced-base for the southern part of the line. General Sir Harold Alexander, who had just assumed executive command of the troops in Tunisia, rushed British troops up from the north and, by threatening Rommel's right flank, prevented any further advance. On 22 February the Germans began to fall back through the Kasserine Pass, and were followed up by the Allies.

Meanwhile General Montgomery, commanding the Eighth Army, had been instructed to make a diversion on his front with the object of relieving the pressure. This he was unfortunately scarcely in a position to do owing to supply difficulties, though he made a slight advance with the 51st Division, which had just reached the front line.

But Rommel was already on his return journey to the Mareth Line, with his ultimate objective—the destruction of the Eighth Army—in view. Fortunately for that Army, the New Zealand Division and 4th Light Armoured Brigade arrived before the attack could be launched, and when it came off on 6 March it was a complete failure. Thereafter Rommel seems to have secretly abandoned all hope of preventing the junction of the two Allied armies.

Meanwhile on 26 February General von Arnim, commanding the Axis forces in Northern Tunisia, launched a series of local attacks against the northern end of the line. On the extreme north they met with considerable success, penetrating by 17 March several miles west of Sedjenane and almost to Beja (Sketch Map 22). If this advance had continued much farther the Allied plans would have been seriously dislocated. But three days later a welcome move was at last made by the Eighth Army.

The battle of the Mareth Line opened on 20 March, and as it contained some instructive features of a semi-strategical nature a brief description of it will be given. The strongest portion of the Mareth Line was known to be on the northern flank near the sea. This had also been the case in the Alamein position occupied by the Axis in the previous autumn. On that occasion General Montgomery had deliberately attacked that strongest point, thereby achieving surprise—and success. He repeated the stratagem here, but not with equal success. For various reasons, including the incalculable element of Chance, the main attack, after a promising start, fared badly. Then came the interesting feature. Montgomery showed not only that ' robustness ' of which Lord Wavell speaks, that will not admit of defeat, but also that flexibility of mind and resource that was such a feature of the Duke of Wellington. He suddenly abandoned his main attack and sent all available armoured units on an immense flank march of two days duration in order to turn the hostile right flank—a good example of the use of exterior lines. Some mounted troops, chiefly New Zealanders, were already on that flank, engaging the Panzers. The armour joined them, and in the evening of 26 March the attack went in. Much confused fighting took place during the next two days, but a big and decisive advance was made which confirmed Rommel in his already contemplated decision to retreat. During the next forty-eight hours he managed with considerable skill, and without undue interference, to disengage from the Mareth Line and to squeeze his whole force through the Gabes Gap (as the passage between Gabes and the salt lakes was called). Montgomery had achieved surprise, as he had done at Alamein, by deliberately attacking the strongest point. Then he showed remarkable flexibility in switching on an entirely different plan. *Flexibility* is so important that it may almost be classed as a Principle of War..

But the attack by the Eighth Army was only a portion of the ambitious plan that General Alexander had contrived. Simultaneously with the attack on the Mareth Line the U.S.A. II Corps north of Gafsa was to join in the attack. This was done, but without much success; the attack was repeated on the 26th with a like result. Thus the retreat of the Axis troops through the ' Gabes Gap ', which it was hoped to bottle up, became possible.

Rommel took up a northern position along the Wadi el Akarit, north of Gabes, defending the gap. He garrisoned it mainly with Italian troops, whilst with two Panzer divisions he tried to repeat his successful operation of a fortnight before. But this time the requisite time and space for the utilization of interior lines were absent. General Montgomery, by strenuous efforts, amassed sufficient ammunition to attack the Akarit position on 6 April. This attack was so successful that Rommel was obliged to abandon both the Akarit Line and his projected attack on the Americans. The latter were still trying, but without much success, to drive in the Axis troops opposite Gafsa, hoping thereby to imperil the retreat of the Axis forces.

Rommel, once having decided to retreat, disengaged, as always, with the utmost speed. Nor did he pause till over 150 miles had been traversed and his force was well

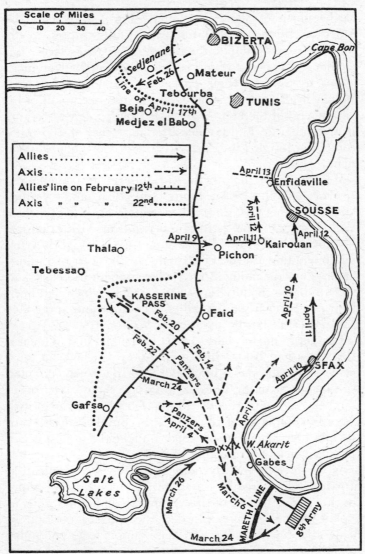

SKETCH MAP 22.—The Tunisian Campaign.

to the north of Sfax. Repeated efforts were made by American, French, and later British units to press in the German western flank, thus cutting off the retreat, but the flank managed to hold sufficiently long for Rommel's troops to continue their retreat to the north of Sousse, though British armour managed to capture the tail of his column east of the Fondouk Pass.[1] On 13 April he came to a stand near Enfidaville, after a retreat of 180 miles from the Mareth Line, and with a loss of about 20,000 men.

Meanwhile in the north Alexander was launching a steady, methodical, but limited offensive, and by mid-April the line was established much as it was before Arnim's attack: that is to say, it ran from Medjez almost due north to the sea. At the same time the Eighth Army had joined up with the First Army to the west of Enfidaville. Thus the moment envisaged six months before had come to pass—the junction of two armies which had been separated by nearly 2,000 miles of country and in the face of a powerful, hostile army.

The last phase had been reached, and General Alexander had before him a situation of which he must have dreamed—a combined force of over 350,000 men working on exterior lines, against an enemy inferior in numbers and with the sea at their back and the British Navy in command of it, and with complete mastery of the air. Sir Harold proceeded to make the utmost use of this strategically favourable situation.

As we have frequently noticed, the correct application of exterior lines involves a simultaneous attack all along the line, in order that the enemy shall not be able to exploit the advantage afforded the interior position of being able to switch forces quickly across from one point to another.

[1] Between Pichon and Kairouan.

But a preliminary operation was necessary. A favourable jumping-off ground was desirable, notably in front of Medjez el Bab—that stout bastion that had resisted all attacks. Here the well-named Longstop Hill was barring the progress of the British 78th Division, and four days' strenuous and bloody fighting was found necessary to clear it. This operation was the most important of several that were taking place. In fact, pressure was being applied all along the line. (See Sketch Map 23—it will be noted that the Americans had been moved, with a portion of the French, to the northern end of the line.) During this phase, which started on 23 April [1] and lasted for twelve days, outward signs of success were comparatively small. But all the time the Allies were steadily wearing down by a process of attrition the inferior resources of the Axis, and reducing Arnim to a state verging on paralysis. His one great concern was to mass the greatest possible strength opposite the dreaded Eighth Army. The best German troops were therefore moved south, leaving the northern sector thinly and comparatively weakly held.

Now Alexander played his trump card. The part played in this general offensive by the Eighth Army appeared small and disappointing; it made but little headway, but General von Arnim dare not remove any of his opposing troops. General Alexander, on the other hand, did. Ordering the Eighth Army to call off its attack, he detached two of its best divisions, the 7th Armoured and the 4th Indian, and marched them round behind General Anderson's First Army. At Medjez el Bab these two divisions joined up with the 4th British and 6th Armoured Divisions of that Army. These four divisions

---

[1] There was very heavy fighting at various points on the preceding days, but it was not continuous all along the line. This day—St. George's Day—was exactly six months since the opening of the battle of Alamein.

were to constitute the hammer which was to deliver the decisive blow.

6 May was the date fixed for this hammer-blow, but a few days previously a surprising development was manifest on the American front opposite Mateur. On 3 May the enemy was found to have vanished, except for a few weak rearguards. The U.S.A. troops followed up cautiously, occupied Mateur, and passed even beyond, encountering at first only a slight resistance. Now, Mateur was a key town forming a connecting link between Bizerta and Tunis. It was the last place the Germans might be expected to give up voluntarily—unless they intended to abandon Bizerta. This, indeed, was Arnim's intention, arrived at about 30 April. The strain on his line had become too great, the line must be shortened, and in order to do this the whole army must withdraw into the Bon Peninsula. A defensive line about fifty miles long had been constructed along its base. Arnim reckoned that inside this line his army could hold out at least till August, by which time the plans of the Allies for the summer's campaign would have been upset.

It was a pretty plan; but it reckoned without Alexander. In its initial stages, however, it seemed to go well. In the face of moderate opposition, the Americans did not penetrate into Bizerta till 7 May, by which time nearly all the Axis troops in that area had side-slipped towards Tunis, en route for the Bon Peninsula. On 6 May the great blow fell. The four divisions were concentrated on a 3,000 yard front: most of the guns were engaged on the creeping barrage—one gun per seven yards of front—just three times as strong as at El Alamein—an unprecedented proportion. A strong force of bombers also joined in the artillery barrage. The effect was almost to blast a hole in the defence. Closely following the barrage, the infantry went forward, the armour leapfrogged through them next morning, and, encountering but slight opposition, pushed right on to Tunis, which was entered thirty-eight hours after the opening of the

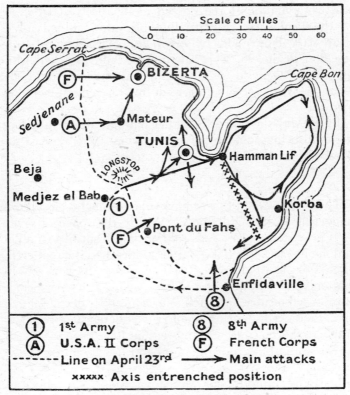

SKETCH MAP 23.—The Battle of Tunis

battle. By this means a large part of the Axis forces were cut off from the Bon Peninsula and tamely surrendered.

But the main body under Arnim was still in the south facing the Eighth Army. It was therefore essential to cut off their retreat to the Bon Peninsula. With this aim the 6th Armoured Division, closely followed by the 4th British, pushed south-east from Tunis, at top speed, crashed through the defensive line near Hamman Lif,[1] whence one force worked south along the line to the sea, while another force moved along the western shore of the Peninsula. Eventually both units joined forces near Cape Bon. The troops in the south, cut off from the Bon Peninsula, were surrounded and attacked from all sides. General von Arnim surrendered, and his example was speedily followed by the remnants of his army.

By 13 May the last Axis soldier had laid down his arms, the total being 290,000. Under 500 escaped by sea—the blockade by the Navy was magnificent.

COMMENTS

The conclusion of this remarkable campaign was almost staggering in its suddenness. Within the space of seven days practically every Axis soldier on a front of 120 miles and in an area of 3,600 square miles had surrendered. (The Navy, assisted by the R.A.F., had done its work so well that only a few hundreds got away by sea.) Never before in recorded history had such a large number of disciplined soldiers cracked so abruptly and surrendered so universally and in so short a time. Many reasons have been suggested for this astonishing phenomenon, and it will be instructive to examine them.

The reason most generally advanced is the effect of the aerial bombardment. No doubt this had a big effect on those troops who were subjected to it; but a glance at the map and a little simple arithmetic should put this factor in its rightful proportions. Now, the front extended for over 120 miles—farther than from London to Bristol.

[1] A captured German general gave it as his opinion that this was the greatest feat of arms of the campaign.

It is fantastic to suppose that in those last few days more than a proportion of Axis troops were in the bombed area; yet ALL of them capitulated. Lest it should be supposed that they were merely obeying, perhaps reluctantly, the orders of General von Arnim, one must recall the conditions under which the German commander capitulated. When the unconditional surrender of his whole army was demanded of him he expostulated that he was out of touch with his units, so could not comply. The logic of this was accepted by us, and he was allowed to surrender personally. Hence it follows that his troops as a whole did NOT receive from him the order to surrender. Yet they ALL did so!

Second reason. The feeling of hopelessness, since the action of our Navy and Air Force had rendered their chances of evacuation improbable. But our troops falling back on Dunkirk did not expect to see England again, yet *they did not surrender as a result.*

Third. Shortage of ammunition. No doubt again the action of our Navy and Air Force was causing this to run short, but it was not completely expended. The famous 10th Panzer Division, according to Alan Moorehead, one of our most reliable war correspondents, ' spend all night shooting away their ammunition, and then in the morning they troop down to the main road, holding white flags aloft '. Further on he states: ' Whole divisions had enough to carry on for a week or two '. There is little of the ' to the last cartridge ' about this.

Fourth. Shortage of food. There is not much evidence of this, though, owing to transport casualties, there were likely to be local shortages. But again let us quote Moorehead (who claims to have seen about 100,000 of them): ' Nearly all the Germans and Italians I have seen were unwounded, well fed, and healthy '.

Fifth. Shortage of supplies such as petrol. This is

more difficult to gauge. Petrol was undeniably running short, a fact of which the Higher Command would be aware, but not necessarily the fighting troops. Yet we hear of one dump of a million gallons being found intact; and we have all heard how some of the Germans still possessed at least enough petrol to drive themselves to the surrender point!

No, none of these reasons singly, nor the whole lot of them taken together, seem to explain the completeness and suddenness of the surrender. Alan Moorehead suggests that the sudden cessation of the flow of orders from above. when Arnim had his communications disorganized, was responsible. 'Like a finely-balanced watch once struck in a vital spot, the whole carefully-geared mechanism ceased running. There was no flexibility.' This is an interesting and attractive theory, and seems preferable to all the preceding ones. But the mere absence of orders in itself could hardly cause the morale of the German soldiers to crack in the way that it evidently did. Some more powerful predisposing cause there must have been. Let us see whether the German surrender in 1918 throws any light on the matter, and let a German, General von Ludendorff, be our witness. This is what he writes in his *Memoirs* respecting the behaviour of the German troops in August 1918: ' I was told of deeds of glorious valour, but also of behaviour which, I openly confess, I should not have thought possible in the German army. Whole bodies of our men had surrendered to single troopers or isolated squadrons. Retiring troops, meeting a fresh division going bravely into action, had shouted out things like " Blacklegs! " and " You are prolonging the war ". 8 August put the decline of that fighting power beyond all doubt. . . . The war must be ended.'

So here we see a sudden crack in morale, not unlike that witnessed in Tunisia. The conclusion seems inescapable. The collapse in 1918 was not due to bombing, nor shortage of food, ammunition supplies, nor the cutting off of their retreat. It was due to the hammer-blows delivered by the Allied armies, and especially by the British Army.

The cause of the *débâcle* in Tunisia was fundamentally the same: *it was the cumulative effect of the succession of hammer-blows delivered by our armies from Alamein onwards.* Sheer hard fighting did it. It was the apotheosis of the offensive. The lesson is clear—there is no short cut to victory—sheer hard fighting, such as our troops employed on Longstop Hill, of glorious memory, in an implacable offensive, is the only sure precursor to victory in war.

Of the many other illustrations of the Art of War that this campaign affords, we will confine our attention to a single one. The campaign is a striking example of the inter-play of Interior and Exterior Lines. The reader should by now be familiar with the factors conducive to success in both cases. Let us see how these factors worked out in the Tunisian campaign.

1. *El Kasserine*. The first blow was struck by Rommel at El Kasserine, and appeared to be completely successful. But Rommel voluntarily retired from the ' bulge ' he had made. Why? Because he correctly appraised the fact that the Allies had no ' ropes ' behind them, and that the farther and deeper he extended the ' bulge ' the more precarious would become his own position. Moreover, he could not be in two places at once, and his real object in attacking the Americans was to keep them at arm's length while he turned on the Eighth Army.

2. *Mareth Line*. *Phase I.* Rommel attacks the Eighth Army. We learn from a captured order that Rommel regarded this attack as the decisive battle of the campaign, for unless he could drive Montgomery right back, the Allies would eventually close in on him. It was, indeed,

decisive in one way—decisive for his own army, but not in the other way—for the Eighth Army; for the latter could retreat 1,500 miles before it reached its ' ropes '; in fact, there were no ' ropes '.

Nevertheless, the above two operations show Rommel at his best; his was the sort of manoeuvre at which Napoleon was an adept. He had ' time and space to manoeuvre ', and he made good use of them. And he attacked only one enemy at a time. But he did not (because he could not) ' deal with his first opponent so drastically as to prevent his return as soon as his back was turned '; in this he repeated Napoleon's great mistake at Leipzig—a mistake that the army working on interior lines will always find it hard to avoid.

3. *Mareth Line, Phase II.* Montgomery made use of a virtue inherent in exterior lines—namely, that he was able to threaten the communications of his opponent without to the same degree exposing his own. Moreover, the very fact that Rommel had two ' ropes ' behind him—the sea and the salt lake—with only a narrow gap between them, made him peculiarly sensitive to such a threat, and induced him to start his withdrawal before even his Italian colleague wished.

4. *Gabes Gap.* Here Rommel tried once more the Napoleonic manoeuvre, throwing his panzers against the Americans. Excellent in theory, if only he had had ' time and space to manoeuvre '. But this time he had neither. Consequently, when Montgomery struck, the Panzers could not get back in time. This is another way of saying that the Eighth Army had strategically joined up with the First Army.

This brought in its train another factor—' good communications '. The next factor—' resolute and bold subordinate commanders '—the Allies already had. There remained but one factor in order to ensure success—

' a continuous attack by all the columns simultaneously '. The word ' simultaneous ' must not be taken too literally; the attacks must be so closely spaced that the enemy has no opportunity to transfer troops from one quiet point to the threatened point in time. This situation or condition of affairs now obtained.

5. *The Final Battle.* The final operations of both armies must be looked upon as *one* operation. Though the pressure and the tempo varied from place to place and time to time, that is the nature of all battles. The essential point is that *simultaneous pressure* was being applied all along the line, all the time. This being so, Arnim could extract no advantage from his central position; he appears to have tried, but it helped to lead to his downfall; for he transferred troops from the American sector to the south when there was no longer time or space for the purpose. For Alexander was now utilizing to the full his ' superior numbers ' (a term which covers superior arms and air armada). All the factors for the decisive success of exterior lines were present, and the inevitable result followed. This was made the easier owing to Arnim continuing his counter-attacks too long, thus delaying his retreat to the Bon Peninsula until it was too late.

It will be noted that in the first and last examples a salient was made by the attacker, but with very different results. This difference emphasizes the essential difference between exterior and interior lines. It may be shown diagrammatically. In Fig. 11, where ABC represents the original line, D represents the salient made by Rommel, and E the salient made by Alexander. In each case there is the same theoretical opportunity for the defender to attack the flanks of the salient thus formed, but there is an important difference. Attacks on the base of the salient D can be made without exposing the communications of the attacker, whereas an attack at the flanks or base of salient *E* (such as at *G*) does expose its own flank to attack. The fact is, the attacker on exterior lines, whilst making a salient of his own at *E*, tends to make two salients in the hostile line at *F* and at *G*, which is not

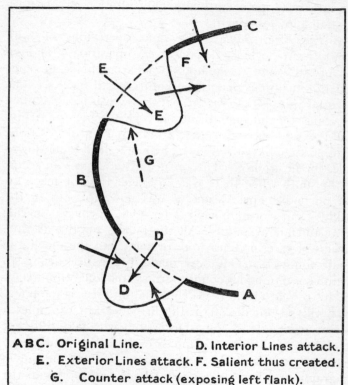

ABC. Original Line.   D. Interior Lines attack.
E. Exterior Lines attack. F. Salient thus created.
G. Counter attack (exposing left flank).

FIG. 11

so in the case of interior lines. This may help to explain why Rommel hastily abandoned his salient at El Kasserine before he was expected to.

But there is a further, and perhaps more powerful, reason why the Germans failed to attack the exposed flanks of Alexander's salient. It was a very narrow one, as the British armour rushed forward to Tunis; German troops were visible on both flanks and an attack was feared; but, so far from attacking, the Germans bolted towards the rear. There can be only one explanation: it was that crack in the German morale which our first comment was at such pains to stress.

Viewed as a whole, whether strategically, tactically, or morally, the Tunisian campaign will doubtless go down to history as a classic. It forms a fitting conclusion to that series of great campaigns ranging from Kadesh in 1288 B.C. to the present day in which the great generals of all ages have forged the Art of War on Land.

EPILOGUE

IT is now time to gather up the threads.

In Part One we propounded the question: What comprises the secret of success in war? And we obtained certain broad answers. We tabulated and analysed the generally accepted principles of war and elements of strategy. In Part Two we traced them in action, and found that these principles are sound, have been sound through the ages, and will probably continue to be so till human nature itself changes.

At the same time we discovered that the effects of these principles are liable to be nullified by certain ' variables ' that cannot be exactly computed in most cases: that, though in the long run in prolonged operations such as the majority of campaigns luck or chance tends to pan out level, in short operations such as battles it is essential to take the element of luck into account. Events might have run a completely different course if the King of the Hittites had not been drowned at Kadesh, if a chance javelin had not struck the charioteer of Darius at Arbela, if the cannon-ball which killed his horse-holder had also struck Marlborough at Ramillies, if French artillery drivers had not elected to graze their horses on the banks of the Scheldt during the battle of Fontenoy, and so on.

We analyzed the factors that determine the strength of armies, and found that they consist of four main elements or strands (of which the strand of leadership is the most important), and we saw that it is the cumulative effect, or teamwork, of these four strands that decides the strength of the blow. At the same time we perceived that it is not absolute but relative strength that is the criterion, that it takes two to make a battle, and that the simile of a tug-of-war was in this connection helpful.

Lastly, and most important of all, we came to see that war is ' an impassioned drama ', not an exact science, and that in the last resort it is the MEN who count—in particular, the Leader of men; that this Leader must be imbued with a resourcefulness and flexibility of mind which will enable him to divert disaster and to improvise victory, with a robustness that will nerve him to gamble and to take risks, recognizing, as Mr. Churchill has told us, that ' nothing is certain in war ', and that he who risks no defeat gains no praiseworthy victory; and, finally, that he must be imbued with that unquenchable spirit which refuses to accept defeat, realizing that, in Marshal Foch's words: ' une bataille gagnée est une bataille ou l'on ne veut pas s'avouer vaincu ', as did our heroic troops on the rocky slopes of Longstop Hill—and the bloody beaches of Salerno.

INDEX

PRINTED IN GREAT BRITAIN BY
RICHARD CLAY AND COMPANY, LTD.,
BUNGAY, SUFFOLK.